P9-DEK-964

Fodor's InFocus

ARUBA

Welcome to Aruba

The pastel houses of Dutch settlers still grace the waterfront in Oranjestad, Aruba's (known as "One Happy Island") capital city. Palm Beach, the island's main tourist hub, is home to beachfront high-rise hotels, dining, shopping, and entertainment. The low-rise hotels, and broadest stretches of white sand, are found along Eagle, Manchebo, and Druif Beaches. Winds are fierce, even savage, on the north coast, where you'll find cacti, rocky desert, and wind-bent divi-divi trees. On the west coast, steady breezes attract windsurfers to the shallow, richly colored waters.

TOP REASONS TO GO

★ **Beaches:** Powdery beaches and turquoise waters or wild waves crashing rocky cliffs.

★ **Nightlife:** Dance-till-you-drop spots and party buses like the Kukoo Kunuku make this island move after dark.

★ **Restaurants:** International fare and local snack hideaways offer foodies much to discover.

★ **Casinos:** Aruba's modern casinos will please both casual and serious gamblers.

★ **The Welcome:** A friendly multilingual population guarantees smiles for everyone.

Contents

MAPS

EXPERIENCE
ARUBA

15 ULTIMATE EXPERIENCES

Aruba offers terrific experiences that should be on every traveler's list. Here are Fodor's top picks for a memorable trip.

1 Awesome Oranjestad

The colorful capital is easily explored on the free Downtown Trolley. Take a downtown walking tour or see free live entertainment at Renaissance Marketplace. *(Ch. 3)*

2 Stunning Eagle Beach

This stunning expanse of powder-soft sand and cerulean sea often tops best beach lists for its sheer beauty and pristine condition. And, it's home to Aruba's iconic tree, so get your selfie sticks ready. *(Ch. 4)*

3 Action-Packed Casinos

If you like to gamble, or want to try your hand at a game or two, Aruba's casinos are the real deal, with options ranging from big, glitzy, Las Vegas–style affairs to intimate little gaming rooms. *(Ch. 3, 4, 5, 8)*

4 San Nicolas Art Walk

Everywhere you look on San Nicolas's main streets, buildings are covered with beautiful murals. The art walk is free to explore on your own, but guided tours are available through Aruba Mural Tours. *(Ch. 6)*

5 Palm Beach Pleasures

One of the world's most popular beaches, Palm Beach is where you'll find many of the Caribbean's most cosmopolitan resorts, deluxe spas, fine restaurants, glittery casinos, and superb swimming. *(Ch.5)*

6 Explore Arikok National Park

Aruba's wild side isn't all parties. Stop by the visitor center and join one of the free guided hikes with a park ranger, or book a jeep tour with DePalm Tours. *(Ch. 7)*

7 Retail Therapy

There are ample opportunities to purchase fine jewelry, quality timepieces, high-end brand name fashions, and Cuban cigars throughout Oranjestad and Palm Beach. *(Ch. 3, 5)*

8 Paseo Herencia

Located on the Palm Beach tourist strip, Paseo Herencia has restaurants, artisan kiosks, and a nightly magical light and water show in its fountain that's worth a visit. *(Ch. 5)*

9 Outstanding Scuba Diving

Advanced and novice divers appreciate the plentiful marine life and abundance of wrecks in Aruba's clear waters. There are even guided night dives, deep dives, and shore dives. *(Ch. 9)*

10 Above-Water Adventures

There are plenty of ways to spend time upon Aruba's aqua waves—party day sails, sunset voyages, dinner cruises, sailing, stand-up paddleboarding, sea kayaking, deep-sea fishing, and Splash Park. (Ch. 9)

11 World-Class Dining

For such a tiny island, Aruba has a large and eclectic food scene: romantic toes-in-the-sand spots, intimate chef's tables, culinary walking tours, or food and wine festivals. (Ch. 3, 4, 5, 6)

12 A Flurry of Festivals

Whether it's food, music, dancing, or art that tickles your fancy, Aruba has a festival for it all. The island's longest-standing event is the weekly Bonbini Festival, but Carnival is the island's biggest celebration. (Ch. 2)

13 Barhopping Buses

Aruba's crazy barhopping buses offer a wild ride replete with stops at popular nightclubs and bars to give visitors a real feel for island nightlife. The bright red Kukoo Kunuku buses are an iconic sight. (Ch. 2)

14 Horseback Riding on Special Steeds

Aruba's rough-and-tumble interior is often best explored on horseback. Some tours lead to interesting landmarks like the ruins of a gold mine, and there are tours for all skill levels and ages. *(Ch. 9)*

15 Superb Snorkeling

With water visibility down to 90 feet, and warm waters full of marine life and colorful coral, snorkelers can often view the same wonders as divers, without the PADI certification. *(Ch. 9)*

WHAT'S WHERE

1 Oranjestad. Aruba's capital is a great place to go for shopping, restaurants, and nightlife.

2 Eagle, Druif, and Manchebo beaches. The island's "low-rise" hotel area offers miles of beautiful beach that's not overdeveloped but is dominated by the sprawling Divi complex.

3 Palm Beach, Noord, and Western Tip. The island's high-rise hotels and condos are found in Palm Beach in the district of Noord. The quiet and remote Western Tip is anchored by the California Lighthouse.

4 Arikok National Park and Environs. Nearly 20% of Aruba is covered by this sprawling national park. The small town of Santa Cruz, in the interior, gives a sense of how real Arubans live.

5 Savaneta and San Nicolas. The bustling fishing village of Savaneta was the first Dutch beachhead on Aruba, while San Nicolas, once headquarters of the island's oil industry, has been reborn with public art.

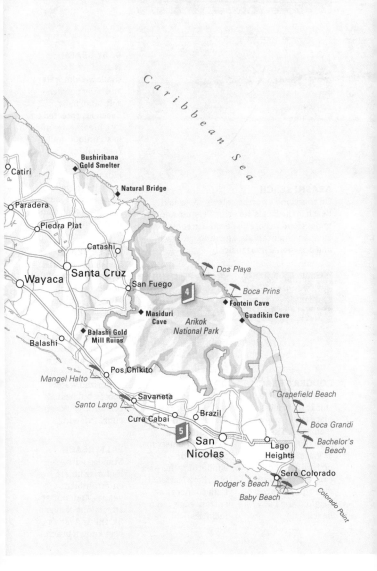

Catiri

Bushiribana
Gold Smelter

Natural Bridge

Paradera

Piedra Plat

Catashi

Wayaca

Santa Cruz

San Fuego

Caribbean Sea

Dos Playa

Boca Prins

Fontein Cave

4

Guadikin Cave

Masiduri
Cave

Arikok
National Park

Balashi Gold
Mill Ruins

Balashi

Pos Chikito

Mangel Halto

Savaneta

Santo Largo

Cura Cabai

Brazil

5

San
Nicolas

Lago
Heights

Grapefield Beach

Boca Grandi

Bachelor's
Beach

Sero Colorado

Rodger's Beach

Baby Beach

Colorado Point

Aruba's Best Beaches

BABY BEACH
Named for its shallow, calm waters and baby powder–soft sand, Baby Beach is protected by a breakwater and has a unique double reef, making it a great place to bring kids or go snorkeling; snorkel gear, lounge chairs, and sunshade tents can be rented.

ARASHI BEACH
On the island's northwestern tip, Arashi Beach is the locals' favorite. Pristine and undeveloped, there's a beach bar, some palapas, chair rentals, an outdoor shower, and occasional live music.

EAGLE BEACH
Consistently listed as one of the world's best beaches, the stunning alabaster soft white sand meets an ever-changing wave of cerulean-hued ocean. There are a few stretches with motorized water sports, but best for romantic walks and sunset viewing.

RODGER'S BEACH
Next to Baby Beach, this is the perfect place to get away from it all. The water is shallow and clear as glass; there are no facilities, but you can rent snorkel or dive equipment at neighboring Baby Beach.

DOS PLAYA
It's not a swimmable spot, but Dos Playa's two beaches, separated by a swathe of limestone, are ideal for sunbathing. It's part of Arikok National Park so there's an entrance fee, but no facilities.

PALM BEACH
Studded with high-rise hotels, entertainment venues, and tourist attractions of every ilk, this is Aruba's best-known beach.

Mangel Halto

Its shallow, clear, pond-calm surf and soft white sand also make it one of the island's best for water sports and young children.

DRUIF BEACH

This lovely half-mile stretch of sand is the main beach for the Divi Aruba All-Inclusive property. Wave action is medium, making it a good place for children, though the surf can be restless at times. There are plenty of food and drink options in the Alhambra Mall.

SURFSIDE BEACH

This little stretch of sand could almost be called an urban beach, as it's very near the heart of downtown Oranjestad. There are chair and umbrella rentals, the small Surf Side Beach Bar with changing facilities, and lovely sunset views.

BOCA CATALINA

Just north of Palm Beach, Boca Catalina is easily accessible by car or public bus. The crystal clear waters make this little cove a favorite among snorkelers, but the beach itself

is small; there are a few public shade palapas, though no chairs or facilities.

MANGEL HALTO

One of Savaneta's best-kept secret snorkel spots, this little cove has a sweet expanse of soft white sand cradled between lush mangrove forests. There are no facilities, but there are a few restaurant-bars nearby and a few public shade palapas.

Aruba's Top Resorts

BUCUTI & TARA BEACH RESORT
This legendary adults-only property on Eagle Beach often tops "most romantic stays in the Caribbean" lists. The Tara Penthouse Suites are the epitome of luxe with deep soaking tubs, spacious balconies, and full kitchens.

THE RITZ-CARLTON ARUBA
The Ritz-Carlton name is synonymous with luxury on every level, but if you're looking to splurge, the penthouse Ritz-Carlton Suite is the island's most pampering perch with a dedicated concierge and personal beach and pool service.

ARUBA OCEAN VILLAS
Secreted away in the tiny village of Savaneta, be prepared for absolute enchantment at this boutique luxury property, a collection of overwater bungalows, stunning beach villas, and even a two-story tree house.

DIVI ARUBA BEACH RESORT AND TAMARIJN ARUBA BEACH RESORT
These side-by-side sister all-inclusives, on the lovely and kid-friendly Druif and Divi Beaches, share access to dining, bars, entertainment, and water sports.

HYATT REGENCY ARUBA RESORT, SPA AND CASINO
Picture this: magnificent faux ruins with a cascading waterfall that empties into a koi pond inhabited by black swans. This scene has always given this Hyatt a distinctively classy character, and the newly refreshed rooms add to its allure.

RENAISSANCE OCEAN SUITES
Located in downtown Oranjestad, the family-friendly property has large suites with kitchens, two pools, and a man-made

Hilton Aruba Caribbean Resort & Casino

beach with a breakwater to keep the surf swimmer-friendly. Plus, there's access to Renaissance Private Island and its famous flamingos.

HOLIDAY INN BEACH RESORT

Located on a stellar stretch of Palm Beach, the super-calm surf and soft sand in front of the sprawling Holiday Inn Beach Resort attracts families in droves, yet never seems crowded. The junior suites are perfect for families since they have small kitchenettes.

DIVI ARUBA PHOENIX BEACH RESORT

Self-caterers love this resort for its communal barbecues and spacious one-, two-, or three-bedroom suites that have an in-room washer/dryer and full kitchens. There's a dedicated children's pool with daily activities, and gentle surf ideal for little ones.

HOTEL RIU PALACE ARUBA

This family-friendly all-inclusive sits on Palm Beach. Kids love the royal Middle Eastern castle design, but the sprawling multi-level water circuit and comprehensive buffet (including a sundae bar and a chocolate fountain) are also big draws.

HILTON ARUBA CARIBBEAN RESORT & CASINO

The spacious beachfront area at the landmark Hilton Aruba is well designed with all kinds of pools and water circuits that lead to lush little tropical nooks, giving one the feeling of ultimate privacy, even if the hotel's at full capacity.

Aruba's Best Outdoor Activities

GREAT GOLFING
Whether you're learning the game or already love it, Aruba has some great courses including the Robert Trent Jones Jr. designed Tierra del Sol, the island's premiere 18-hole golf course.

SNORKEL OR SEA KAYAK
With calm, clear aqua waters teeming with tropical fish, there's plenty to see under the waves, including numerous shipwrecks. You can snorkel or take a guided sea kayaking tour; one option includes glass-bottomed kayaks that light up the waters.

SCUBA DIVING
Aruba is known among divers as the Caribbean's wreck capital, and there are plenty of dive sites right offshore, some in very shallow water, that have helped the island earn its reputation. The island also has plenty of dive operators for novice and expert divers.

OFFBEAT BLOKARTING
Aruba's constant winds and abundance of flat land make it one of the few places where you can try blokarting (a.k.a land sailing); Aruba Active Vacations is the only operator to offer it. Prepare to get dusty and dirty; wear sunglasses.

EXPLORE BY BIKE
The paved Linear Park—from downtown Oranjestad to the airport—has made biking very popular. Explore it on rentable electric bikes or through the island's bike share program; some resorts provide free coaster bikes.

OFF-ROADING EXPLORATIONS
Aruba's interior is rugged and rocky and best explored with an ATV, especially if you want to explore the cacti-studded

Windsurfing and kiteboarding

countryside or visit incredible landmarks like the small natural bridges or the wild coast. Tours can be booked with De Palm Tours and ABC Tours.

ARIKOK PARK HIKING

Explore the island's arid outback with a guided tour to unearth all the secrets of the park. Start at the park's visitor center; there's a small museum, café, and maps, and it's where the free, but short, park ranger–guided tours of the immediate area leave.

HORSEBACK RIDING

Aruba has an interesting equine history that starts with Spanish explorers. There are trails and rides for all ages through interesting terrain like goldmine ruins and cacti-studded outback as well as along sand dunes and beautiful beaches.

WINDSURFING AND KITEBOARDING

With shallow waters and constant gentle winds, the conditions at Fishmen's Huts Beach (a.k.a

Hadicuari) are ideal for beginner windsurfers. Boca Grandi is a favorite hangout for kiteboarders, and the annual Aruba Hi-Winds event attracts international talent.

DAY SAILS

There are party boats, classy dinner cruises, and romantic sunset sails to enjoy, and even authentic wooden pirate ships with rope swings to try some aerial acrobatics on your way into the waves.

Aruba Today

Arubans are proud of their autonomous standing within the Kingdom of the Netherlands, and Gilberto François "Betico" Croes is heralded as the hero behind the island's *status aparte* (separate status). His birthday, January 25, is an official Aruban holiday.

During the Dutch colonial expansion of the 17th century, Aruba and five other islands—Bonaire, Curaçao, St. Maarten, St. Eustatius, and Saba—became territories known as the Netherlands Antilles. After World War II these islands began to pressure Holland for autonomy, and in 1954 they became a collective self-governing entity under the umbrella of the Kingdom of the Netherlands.

At that time, several political parties were in power on the island. Soon, however, Juancho Irausquin (who has a major thoroughfare named in his honor) formed a new party that maintained control for nearly two decades. Irausquin was considered the founder of Aruba's new economic order and the precursor of modern Aruban politics. After his death his party's power diminished.

In 1971 Croes, then a young, ambitious school administrator, became the leader of another political party. Bolstered by a thriving economy generated by Aruba's oil refinery, Croes spearheaded the island's cause to secede from the Netherlands Antilles and to gain status as an equal partner within the Dutch kingdom. Sadly, he didn't live to celebrate the realization of his dream. On December 31, 1985, the day before Aruba's new status became official, Croes was in a car accident that put him in a coma for 11 months. He died on November 26, 1986. Etched in the minds of Arubans are his prophetic words: *Si mi cai na cominda, gara e bandera y sigui cu e lucha* ("If I die along the way, seize the flag and go on with the struggle").

On March 18, 1948, the Aruban politician Shon A. Eman put forth the first formal proposal for Aruba's independence from the Netherlands Antilles. Twenty-eight years later to the day, Croes declared the first National Anthem and Flag Day, a national holiday that celebrates Aruba's independence with parades, sporting and cultural events, and lots of food. Most shops, gas stations, and supermarkets are closed or close early.

Aruba has its own democratic constitution and its capital is in Oranjestad. The parliament consists of 21 elected members; the majority parties form a seven-member Council of Ministers that's headed by a prime minister for a four-year term. The reigning monarch of the Netherlands appoints a governor who holds office for a six-year term, and acts as her representative. In 2017, Aruba made history in appointing its first female prime minister, Evelyn Wever-Croes.

Today, the country is fairly stable, and the struggle is more about preserving the island's environmental legacy. Welcoming over 2 million visitors a year has taken a toll on the island's fragile ecosystem, and the government has been aggressive in passing laws to protect it. As of 2017, plastic bags were banned, and as of January 2019, plastic straws and cutlery and Styrofoam take-away containers and plates were also legally banned. The use of sunscreen that contains oxybenzone—very harmful to the coral reefs—is also against the law.

Aruba with Kids

Aruba has a kid-loving culture, and its slogan "One Happy Island" extends to young visitors as well. The island is a reasonably short flight away from most of the Eastern Seaboard (about three to six hours). Though the island may not offer all of the distractions of a theme-park holiday, it has more than enough to keep most kids occupied during a family vacation.

WHERE TO STAY

Virtually all the best places for families to stay are on or along the beaches that run the length of the western side of the island. An ocean view isn't a necessity, but ease of access to one of the beaches is recommended.

Best High-Rise Resorts. Choose a high-rise resort if you want a great variety of amenities and activities; most offer kids' programs or dedicated kids' clubs. The **Hyatt Regency Aruba Beach Resort** offers an extensive kids' program and has many family-fun activities, and the **Ritz-Carlton Aruba** has the Ritz Kidz program with seriously creative activities inspired by Jean-Michel Cousteau (Jacques Cousteau's son) and his Ocean Futures Society. **Holiday Inn Aruba** has a great dedicated kids' club and a family fun zone, too.

Best Low-Rise Resorts. Low-rise resorts are mostly found along Eagle Beach, Manchebo Beach, and Druif Beach and are often less crowded. The smaller properties may not offer as many amenities and water sports as the high-rises, but they provide a relaxing, laid-back vibe, and some do have kids' programs. **Amsterdam Manor** on Eagle Beach is a good-value hotel with kitchenettes and a mini–grocery store on-site. At **Divi and Tamarijn Aruba All-Inclusives** on Druif Beach, children under 12 stay free when accompanied by two adults, and their kids' camp even offers Papiamento language lessons. Divi Dutch Village offers families spacious suites with full kitchens and laundry facilities, and now also offers an all-inclusive option. The beach there is gorgeous, and all nonmotorized water sports are included in the price. The Divi resorts also have a 30-foot-tall climbing tower on the beach.

BEACHES

Palm Beach is wide and offers powdery white sand, very calm waters, and plenty of nearby amenities like food and beverages. Families that want to avoid the crowds might find **Druif** and **Manchebo** beaches more to their liking, but there aren't as many options for chair rentals, refreshments, or water sports. Sprawling **Eagle Beach** has fewer crowds and a large range of amenities within easy walking distance, but surf can be rough at times and the current strong, so take care with little ones there. Just outside of San Nicolas, Baby Beach—aptly named for its kid-friendly surf and protected pool of shallows waters—is worth a day away from the resorts.

WATER ACTIVITIES

Snorkeling, swimming, kayaking, and sailing are some of the things that keep families coming back to Aruba. Most hotels and condos offer inexpensive equipment rentals for a day in the water. Seasoned junior snorkelers will find the viewing pretty dull off the major beaches, so organized tours such as those offered by **De Palm Tours** and **Red Sail Sports,** and **Jolly Pirates,** which explores more remote coves, may provide a better underwater experience, plus they all stop at the massive Antilla Wreck in shallow water so kids can see it without diving. **De Palm Island** offers a variety of water activities for kids, including snorkeling and a water park that makes for a great day in the sun.

Though a bit pricey for larger families, the **Atlantis Submarine Tour** will likely entertain even the most jaded teen.

Splash Park right downtown is the latest fun-filled family attraction on the water.

LAND ACTIVITIES

The **Aruba Ostrich Farm** is short excursion, while Philip's Animal Garden is where kids will be entertained for hours by its many fun creatures and a huge playground. **The Butterfly Farm** is also a lovely experience for all ages, and if you go early in your holiday, you can return for free as many times as you want with your original admission voucher. The **Donkey Sanctuary Aruba** is also a must-visit. (Bring apples and carrots!) And for evening activities, Paseo Herencia has a gorgeous waltzing waters show three times a night in their amphitheater-courtyard, and a carousel and small train. They also often have cultural shows and bouncy castles for kids, and there are movie cinemas there as well. Palm Beach Plaza Mall right behind it also has glow-in-the-dark bowling, movies, a huge video arcade, and a food court.

Chowing Down Aruban Style

Arubans like their food spicy, and that's where the island's famous Madame Janette sauce comes in handy. It's made with Scotch bonnet peppers (similar to habanero peppers), which are so hot, they can burn your skin when they're broken open. Whether they're turned into *pika,* a relishlike mixture made with papaya, or sliced thin into vinegar and onions, these peppers are sure to set your mouth ablaze. Throw even a modest amount of Madame Janette sauce into a huge pot of soup, and your taste buds will tingle. (Referring to the sauce's spicy nature, Aruban men often refer to an attractive woman as a "Madame Janette.") ■TIP➜ **To tame the flames, don't go for a glass of water, as capsaicin, the compound in peppers that produces the heat, isn't water soluble. Dairy products (especially), sweet fruits, and starchy foods such as rice and bread are the best remedies.**

If you're interested in tasting other food that's unique to the Dutch- and Caribbean-influenced island, then you ought to try one of these local treats.

Balashi: After a day at the beach there's nothing better than sipping a nice, cold Balashi, Aruba's national beer and the only beer brewed on the island. The taste of Balashi is comparable to a Dutch pilsner.

Bitterballen: Crispy bite-size meatballs, which are breaded and then deep-fried, make for the perfect savory snack or appetizer. Dip them in a side of mustard, and wash them down with a cold beverage.

Cocada: Bite-size pieces of these sweet coconut candies are typically served on a coconut shell.

Funchi: This classic Aruban cornmeal side dish is eaten at all times of day and is commonly served with soup.

Keshi Yena: A traditional Aruban dish made with chicken, beef, or seafood in a rich brown sauce of spices and raisins, keshi yena is served with rice in a hollowed-out Gouda cheese rind.

Kesio: This popular dessert is essentially a custard flan or crème caramel.

Pan Bati: The slightly sweet pancakes are commonly eaten as a side with meat, fish, or soup entrées.

Pan Dushi: Delectable little raisin bread rolls are *dushi,* which is Papiamento for "sweet."

Pastechi: Aruba's favorite fast food is an empanadalike fried pastry filled with spiced meat, fish, or cheese.

Carnival

From New Year's Day to the first week in March, Aruba offers its biggest cultural celebration, incorporating local traditions with those of Venezuela, Brazil, Holland, and North America. Trinidadians who came to work at the oil refinery in the 1940s introduced Carnival and steel-pan music to the island; the instruments were originally made from old oil drums.

The monthlong celebration swings between Oranjestad and San Nicolas with pageants, parades, musical competitions, ceremonies, and gala concerts. Local dressmakers turn out the best costumes for parade days as well as the annual carnival queen competition and pageants. Locals look forward to the Lighting Parade, a nighttime parade held in February that lights up the streets. The weeks in between, Aruba has many street parades, locally called "jump-ups," that lead up to the major parade in early March, including San Nicolas's Jouvert Morning Jump-Up (also called the Pajama Party, since it begins at 4 am and many people come straight from bed). The Grand Parade, as it is called, is held on the Sunday before Ash Wednesday for two days, first in San Nicolas and then in the capital city, Oranjestad, with thousands dancing in the streets and viewing the floats, costumes, and bands; it's the largest and longest carnival parade held on the ABC islands. All events end on Shrove Tuesday: at midnight an effigy of King Momo (traditionally depicted as a fat man) is burned to signal the end of the season.

If you can't make it to Carnival, head to San Nicolas at 7 pm on the Wednesday of the last week of each month to get a taste of the festival's spirit. Island Festival showcases the best of the celebration's color and costumes, music, art, and local food and drink. It's an excellent street party that also gives you a chance to view all the new outdoor art that has taken over San Nicolas, the tiny town where Carnival began.

There's also a new *Carnival Euphoria* exhibition in San Nicolas with costumes and art displays that is slated to become a permanent carnival museum in 2020.

Aruba Shopping 101

Of course, there are typical souvenir choices in Aruba like baseball caps, refrigerator magnets, T-shirts, and key chains, but if you take the time to look, you can find items that were made on Aruba. Seek out the **Local Market** near the cruise ship terminal for great take-home items made by island artists and crafters. ■TIP➜ **It's not the string of flea market vendors along the marina; it's a stand-alone area of tents just across from the cruise terminal. Look for the big red chair.**

LOCAL ARTS AND CRAFTS

For high-quality arts and crafts made by local artisans, head to Cosecha (⊕ *www.arubacosecha.com*), housed in a big yellow building Downtown, or its sister organization, Cosecha Creative Centre, in San Nicolas. Products featured in Cosecha have been given the SEYO national seal of craftsmanship, and both locations sell quality handmade items; the San Nicolas outlet hosts craft workshops. Many major resorts also host events where they invite local artisans to come and sell their wares on their property; check with the hotel's information desk for times. Handmade jewelry made from local sea glass is always a highlight at these affairs as well, and sometimes local artist Gaby Gonzalez of Aruba's Hands is

on-site demonstrating how to blow glass.

ECO-CONSCIOUS SOUVENIRS

Aruba outlawed plastic shopping bags in 2017. If you need a bag to carry your treasures, look for Arubiano (⊕ *arubiano. com*) grocery bags that feature iconic Aruban scenes shot by internationally known local photographer, Damilice Mansur; the company also sells flip-flops and hats with Aruba scenes on them. Not only are the bags made from recycled content, but part of the proceeds are donated to the local Aruba Birdlife Conservation foundation.

SHOPPING THAT GIVES BACK

American expat Jodi Tobman moved to Aruba in the 1990s and opened a chain of unique retail stores including The Juggling Fish (⊕ *www. arubaswimwear.com*), The Lazy Lizard (⊕ *www.thelazylizard. com*), and T.H. Palm and Co. (⊕ *www.thpalmandcompany. com*), which can be found in both the high-rise and low-rise hotel sectors. Her shops are well-known among local and repeat visitors for having some of the island's most interesting finds, as Tobman travels the globe seeking out unique products to stock the stores with items like home goods, clothing, and jewelry, always with an eye toward hand-crafted or sustainable or arty concepts. But, possibly most importantly, these stores are part of a community give-back program called Tikkun Olam—loosely translated as "repair the world" in Hebrew—which donates a percentage of every purchase made in its stores to a local nonprofit of the buyer's choice.

LOCAL PRODUCTS

This happy island produces some of the world's finest aloe, and it's home to the world's oldest aloe company. Founded in 1890, Aruba Aloe Balm N.V. was one of the first companies to create and produce aloe-based skin-, hair-, and sun-care products. There are shops at the airport, cruise terminal, and at various locations along Palm Beach, Eagle Beach, and Oranjestad. You can also visit the Aruba Aloe Museum, Factory, and Store in Hato for a free guided tour that explains how aloe is harvested and produced; tours are given in English, Dutch, and Spanish every 15 minutes, seven days a week. The museum has exhibits on the history of the company as well as an 11-minute movie about the brand, and there's a shop on-site.

TRAVEL SMART ARUBA

Updated by
Sue Campbell

★ **CAPITAL:**
Oranjestad

👫 **POPULATION:**
35,000

💬 **LANGUAGE:**
Dutch, Papiamento

$ **CURRENCY:**
Aruban florin (AWG)

📞 **AREA CODES:**
297

⚠ **EMERGENCIES:**
911

🚗 **DRIVING:**
On the right

⚡ **ELECTRICITY:**
110 volts (same as U.S.)

🕐 **TIME:**
Atlantic Standard Time (same as the East Coast)

🌐 **WEBSITES:**
www.aruba.com

What to Know Before You Go

Should you tip in Aruba? If so, to whom and how much? Can you drink the water? Do people speak English or Dutch? Can you use American money, or should you exchange money? Does the island get hurricanes? We've got answers and a few tips to help you make the most of your visit.

WHAT'S THE WEATHER LIKE?

Aruba doesn't really have a rainy season and it's outside of the hurricane belt—one reason why the island is more popular than most during the off-season from mid-May through mid-November, when the risk of Atlantic hurricanes is at its highest. Temperatures are constant (along with the trade winds) year-round. Expect daytime temperatures in the 80s Fahrenheit and nighttime temperatures in the high 70s. Tradewinds blow constantly at an average of 20 knots.

DO AMERICANS NEED A PASSPORT OR VISA?

A valid passport is required to enter or reenter the United States from Aruba.

U.S. tourists do not need a visa to travel to Aruba.

SHOULD YOU TIP?

Most restaurants add a service charge of 15%. It's not necessary to tip once a service charge has been added to the bill, but sometimes that tip is shared between all staff. If the service is good, an additional tip of 10% is always appreciated. If no service charge is included on the final bill, then leave the customary tip of 15% to 20%.

DON'T EXPECT LUSH GREENERY

Aruba is not a lush tropical island, and there are no rain forests. In fact, the island only averages 20 inches of rainfall per year. Beyond the palms transplanted on Palm Beach, there's very little greenery. The interior is arid and desertlike, and cacti, aloe, and divi-divi trees are the few plants hardy enough to survive and thrive.

IT'S OKAY TO DRINK THE WATER

Aruba's drinking water is among the safest and best tasting in the world and it comes from desalinated sea water. The local beer is also made from desalinated seawater.

NEW GREEN LAWS AFFECT SHOPPING

Aruba has passed some very forward-thinking environmental laws in the last few years. Plastic bags, Styrofoam plates, and plastic straws have been banned, so bring your own reusable shopping bag or buy a souvenir one there.

U.S. DOLLARS ARE FINE

You probably won't need to change any money if you're coming from the United States. American currency is accepted everywhere in Aruba, though you might get some change back in local currency—the Aruban florin, also called the guilder—at smaller, out-of-the-way stores.

THERE'S LOTS TO DO AFTER DARK

Beyond offering idyllic fun-in-the-sun days on gorgeous beaches, Aruba is renowned for its vibrant nightlife and glitzy casinos, most within easy walking distance of each other. The legal drinking and gambling age is 18, though there are a few exceptions where over 21 is the rule.

YES, THERE IS TRAFFIC

Oranjestad traffic can be heavy during rush hour. Allow a bit of extra time if you're trying to get into town for a dinner reservation or need to get to the airport at an appointed time. If you rent a car, expect to have some issues with the island's multitude of roundabouts until you get used to them.

EVERYONE SPEAKS ENGLISH

Most Arubans speak at least four languages—English, Spanish, Papiamento, and Dutch. With the odd exception of domestic staff from Latin America working in the large resorts, you'll have no problem finding someone who speaks English.

ADDRESSES ARE INFORMAL

"Informal" might best describe Aruban addresses. Sometimes the street designation is in English (as in J. E. Irausquin Boulevard), other times in Dutch (as in Wilhelminastraat); sometimes it's not specified whether something is a boulevard or a *straat* (street) at all. Street numbers follow street names, and postal codes aren't used. In rural areas you might have to ask a local for directions—and be prepared for such instructions as "Take a right at the market, then a left where you see the big divi-divi tree."

ECO-FRIENDLY SUNSCREEN IS A MUST

The sun is very strong, and the trade winds can trick you into thinking you're not getting burned, so sunscreen is a must. However, Aruba has also passed a law against sunscreen that contains the coral-harming chemical oxybenzone, so check that yours does not, or buy some eco-friendly screen when on island.

EXPECT TO RETURN

Don't stress if you don't get to do everything you want. Chances are good you'll be back, as Aruba has the highest repeat visitor ratio in the entire Caribbean (65%).

Getting Here and Around

Aruba is a small island, so it's virtually impossible to get lost when exploring. Most activities take place in and around Oranjestad or in the two main hotel areas, which are designated as the "low-rise" and "high-rise" areas. Main roads on the island are generally excellent, but getting to some of the more secluded beaches or historic sites will involve driving on unpaved tracks. Though Aruba is typically a very arid island, there can be occasional periods of heavy rain, and it's best to avoid exploring the national park or other wilderness areas during these times, since roads can become flooded, and muddy conditions can make driving treacherous.

Air

Aruba is 2½ hours from Miami; 4½ hours from New York; 5 hours from Boston, Chicago, Atlanta, or Toronto. Smaller airlines connect the Dutch islands in the Caribbean, often using Aruba as a hub; it's a ¼- to ½-hour hop (depending on whether you take a prop or a jet plane) from Curaçao to Aruba.

AIRPORTS

The island's Queen Beatrix International Airport (AUA) has been recently revamped and is equipped with thorough security, lots of flight displays, and state-of-the-art baggage-handling systems, shopping, and food-and-drink emporiums. There's also airportwide free Wi-Fi and new VIP club lounges and services.

GROUND TRANSPORTATION

A taxi from the airport to most hotels takes about 20 minutes (traffic depending). It costs about $26 to hotels along Eagle Beach, $31 to the high-rise hotels on Palm Beach, and $21 to hotels downtown. You'll find a taxi stand right outside the baggage-claim area. Aruba taxis are not metered; they operate on a flat rate by destination. See ⊕ www.aruba.com/things-to-do/taxis-and-limousine-services for more information on rates.

For a PDF of rates see ⊕ www.aruba.com/sigma/Aruba_Taxi_Fares.pdf.

FLIGHTS

Many airlines fly nonstop to Aruba from several cities in North America; connections are usually at a U.S. airport.

There are nonstop flights from Atlanta (Delta), Baltimore (Southwest), Boston (American, JetBlue, US Airways), Charlotte (American), Chicago (United), Fort Lauderdale (Spirit, JetBlue), Houston (Southwest, United), Miami (American, Aruba Airlines), Newark

(United), Minneapolis (Delta), New York–JFK (American, Delta, JetBlue), New York–Newark (United), Orlando (Southwest), Philadelphia (American), and Washington, D.C.–Dulles (United). Seasonal nonstops from major Canadian cities are available from WestJet and Air Canada and charter airlines like Sunwing and Air Transat.

Because of pre-U.S. customs clearance, you really need three hours before departure from Aruba's airport. Beyond typical check-in lines—unless you check-in online and do not have baggage—you must go through two separate security checks and customs as well, and sometimes even random baggage checks. The entire procedure takes a lot of time, and often there are not enough customs agents on duty to handle all the traffic, especially on weekends. So be there early. The good news is that you do not have to deal with customs in the United States on the other end. The airport departure tax is included in the price of your ticket.

🚲 Bicycle

Since the construction of the island's paved Linear Park, which lines the coast from downtown Oranjestad to the airport, casual cycling has become a big deal on Aruba. There's a new bike sharing program, Green Bike, that makes it easy to hop on one of the 100 bicycles distributed throughout eight different stations around the island. You can rent electric bicycles at Aruba BikeTours or motocycles from Aruba Motorcycle Tours. Some resorts also offer their guests complimentary coaster bikes to pedal around on.

Bus

Arubus N.V. is Aruba's public transportation company. Island buses are clean, well maintained, sometimes air-conditioned, and regularly scheduled; they provide a safe, economical way to travel along the resort beaches all the way to downtown Oranjestad main terminal. They stop at almost all major resorts and are a great way to hop into town for groceries to bring back to your hotel without taking expensive taxis. They run until fairly late at night and later on weekends. If you plan to take multiple trips in one day, purchase a day pass for US$10 at the main terminal in downtown Oranjestad for unlimited access to all their routes. Drivers give change if you don't have the exact fare (no large bills, though) and

Getting Here and Around

accept U.S. currency (but give change in florins). A one-way fare is US$2.60, and you can buy a return (round-trip) to Oranjestad for $5. Return bus fares to San Nicolas and Baby Beach from downtown are $8. Get all the updated information on rates, schedules, and routes on their website because things change often.

Car

Driving is on the right, just as in the United States. Most of Aruba's major attractions are fairly easy to find, and there are great maps all over the island to find out-of-the-way spots (mapping apps can also help). International traffic signs and Dutch-style traffic signals (with an extra light for a turning lane) can be confusing, though, if you're not used to them; use extreme caution, especially at intersections, until you grasp the rules of the road.

GASOLINE
Gas prices average a little more than $1.06 a liter (roughly a quarter of a gallon), which is reasonable by Caribbean standards but more expensive than in the United States. Stations are plentiful in and near Oranjestad, San Nicolas, and Santa Cruz, and near the major high-rise hotels on the west coast. All take cash, and

most take major credit cards. Nevertheless, gas prices aren't posted prominently, since they're fixed and the same at all stations.

PARKING
Parking downtown can be a challenge, but Oranjestad has recently introduced Aruparking—a collection of metered spots around the downtown core—and there is free parking behind the Renaissance Marketplace. Arupark meters accept local and U.S. coins, and some accept credit cards, but if you're going to park downtown frequently, it's best to get a rechargeable Smart-Card or download the iParkMe app to pay. Smart Cards are available at most stores and car rental kiosks and can be topped up at Aruparking and Arubus recharging stations.

RENTAL CARS
In Aruba you must meet the minimum age requirements of each rental service. (Budget, for example, requires drivers to be over 25; Avis, over 23). A credit card (with a sufficient line of credit available) or a cash deposit of $500 is required. Rates vary seasonally and are usually lower from local agencies, but shopping for bargains and reserving a car online is a good strategy regardless of which company you rent from. Insurance is

available starting at about $10 per day. Most visitors pick up their rental car at the airport, where you'll find both local and international brands; most companies have offices right across the road from the airport exit (⊕ *www.airportaruba.com/car-rental*), but there are branches all over the island, including at major resorts. Most companies offer free drop-off and pickup at your hotel if you aren't renting a car on arrival. You can ask the concierge of your hotel or the front desk to recommend a local rental if you only want one for a day to tour the island. Opt for a four-wheel-drive vehicle if you plan to explore the outback and go off the beaten path.

RENTAL-CAR INSURANCE

Everyone who rents a car wonders whether the insurance that the rental companies offer is worth the expense. No one—including us—has a simple answer. If you own a car, your personal auto insurance may cover a rental to some degree, though not all policies protect you abroad; always read your policy's fine print. If you don't have auto insurance, then seriously consider buying the collision- or loss-damage waiver (CDW or LDW) from the car-rental company, which eliminates your liability for damage to the car. Some credit cards offer CDW coverage, but

it's usually supplemental to your own insurance and rarely covers SUVs, minivans, or luxury models. If your coverage is secondary, you may still be liable for loss-of-use costs from the car-rental company. But no credit-card insurance is valid unless you use that card for *all* transactions, from reserving to paying the final bill. It's sometimes cheaper to buy insurance as part of your general travel-insurance policy.

ROADSIDE EMERGENCIES

Discuss with the rental-car agency what to do in the case of an emergency. Make sure you understand what your insurance covers and what it doesn't; let someone at your accommodations know where you're heading and when you plan to return. Keep emergency numbers with you, just in case. Because Aruba is such a small island, you should never panic if you have car trouble; it's likely you'll be within relatively easy walking distance of a populated area unless you're in the national park, so have your phone charged at all times.

ROAD CONDITIONS

Aside from the major highways, some of the island's winding roads are poorly marked (although the situation is slowly improving). Keep an eye out for rocks and other

Getting Here and Around

debris when driving on remote roads. When in the countryside, also keep your eyes open for wild goats and donkeys that might wander onto the road.

RULES OF THE ROAD

Driving here is on the right side of the road, American-style. Despite the laid-back ways of locals, when they get behind the steering wheel they often speed and take liberties with road rules, especially outside the more heavily traveled Oranjestad and hotel areas. Keep a watchful eye for passing cars and for vehicles coming out of side roads. Speed limits are rarely posted, but the maximum speed is 60 kph (40 mph) and 40 kph (25 mph) through settlements. Speed limits and the use of seat belts are enforced.

 Taxi

You'll find taxis at the airport and also at all major resorts (ask if you need one to be called). You don't really hail cabs in Aruba; if you need one, just go to the nearest hotel, and the doorman will get you one. Your restaurant or bar will also call one for you. In downtown Oranjestad, taxis are always to be found around the Renaissance Marina lower lobby. Taxi rates in Aruba are fixed (i.e., there are no meters; the rates are set by the government and displayed on a chart by zone) and are posted on the Aruba Tourism Authority website and the Aruba airport website, though you should confirm the fare with your driver before your ride begins. Minimum fare is US$7. There is an additional $3 charge to regular fares from 11 pm to 7 am and on some holidays. Be forewarned that taxi drivers will not allow anyone in wet bathing suits or wet shorts in their vehicles.

Essentials

Activities

Since soft, sandy beaches and turquoise waters are the biggest draws in Aruba, they can be crowded. Eagle Beach is the less crowded of the main ones and the best the island has to offer for postcard-perfect scenery. Diving is also good in Aruba; there are many wrecks to explore.

Near-constant breezes and tranquil, protected waters have proven to be a boon for windsurfers and kiteboarders, who have discovered that conditions on the southwestern coast are ideal for their sport.

A largely undeveloped region in Arikok National Park is the destination of choice for visitors wishing to hike and explore some wild terrain.

🏖 Beaches

The beaches on Aruba are legendary: the solid 7 miles of beachfront along its west coast are baby-powder-soft, blindingly white sand carpets that smile over vast expanses of clear azure water with varying degrees of surf action. The waters of Palm Beach in front of the high-rise resort strip are typically pond-still placid, whereas the waves on the low-rise resort strip on

Eagle Beach are typically restless and rolling. The beaches on the northeastern side are unsafe for swimming because of strong currents and rough swells, but they are worth seeking out for their natural beauty and romantic vistas. You might see bodyboarders and kitesurfers out there, but they are typically highly skilled locals who know the conditions well. Swimming on the sunrise side of the island is best done in Savaneta at Mangel Halto and in San Nicolas at Rodger's Beach or Baby Beach, named for its toddler-friendly calm waters.

Dining

There are a few hundred restaurants on Aruba, from elegant eateries to seafront shacks, so you're bound to find something to tantalize your taste buds. You can sample a wide range of cuisines—Italian, French, Argentine, Asian, Peruvian, and Cuban, to name a few—reflecting Aruba's extensive blend of cultures. And due to the large number of repeat tourists from the United States, American-style fare is everywhere, too. But chefs have to be creative on this tiny island because of the limited number of locally grown ingredients; beyond fresh fish

Essentials

and seafood, much has to be imported. Many are getting much better at providing farm-to-fork menus when possible and catering to restricted diets like gluten-free and vegan. Hot sauce made from local Madame Janette peppers is on local tables, and the seafood du jour is always a good choice just about everywhere.

Although most resorts offer better-than-average dining, don't be afraid to try one of the many excellent independent places. Ask locals about their favorite spots; some of the lesser-known restaurants offer food that's reasonably priced and definitely worth sampling. Most restaurants on the western side of the island are along Palm Beach or in downtown Oranjestad, both easily accessible by taxi or bus. If you're heading to a restaurant in Oranjestad for dinner, leave about 15 minutes earlier than you think you should; in-town traffic can get busy once beach hours are over. Some restaurants in Savaneta are worth the trip; spring for a cab if you intend to be drinking their great cocktails and wine. Breakfast lovers are in luck as most resorts have bountiful breakfast buffets, and you can't go wrong at Dutch Pancakehouse at any time of day. For a fabulous Sunday brunch, Windows on Aruba is the

place to be. The entire month of October is now "Eat Local Restaurant Month" with lots of events and specials island-wide at participating restaurants.

The island is also a particularly family-friendly destination, so bringing the kids along is rarely a problem, and many restaurants offer children's menus.

Enjoy discounts on many of Aruba's finest restaurants when you participate in this association's comprehensive "Aruba Dining" programs. Choose from a wide range of options that include complimentary extras like desserts, appetizers, and more. You can book your package ahead online on their website. You can also order gift certificates for them to be delivered directly to the recipient's hotel.

Unless otherwise noted, the restaurants listed in this guide are open daily for lunch and dinner.

ARUBAN CUISINE

Aruba shares many of its traditional foods with Bonaire and Curaçao. These dishes are a fusion of the various influences that have shaped the culture of the islands. Proximity to mainland South America means that many traditional snack and breakfast foods of Venezuelan origin, such as empanadas, have been adopted into local eats; on Aruba they are called *"pastechis"* and come with a wide variety of fillings. The Dutch influence is evident in the fondness for cheese of all sorts, but especially Gouda. *Keshi yena,* ground meat or seafood with seasonings placed in a hollowed-out cheese rind before baking, is a national dish. Arubans also love their *bolos* (cakes), so look for local favorites like cashew nut, pistachio, or chocolate rum cake.

If there's one thread that unites the cuisines of the Caribbean, it's cornmeal, and Arubans love nothing more than a side of *funchi* (like a thick polenta) or a *pan bati* (a fried cornmeal pancake) to make a traditional meal complete. Though Aruban cuisine isn't by nature spicy, it's almost always accompanied by a small bowl of spicy *pika* (a condiment of fiery hot peppers and onions in vinegar) or a bottle of hot sauce made from local peppers. An abundance of fish means that seafood is the most popular protein on the island, and it's been said that if there were an Aruban national dish, it would be the catch of the day.

PRICES AND DRESS
Aruba's elegant restaurants—where you might have to dress up a little (jackets for men, sundresses for women)—can be pricey. If you want to spend fewer florins, opt for the more casual spots, where being comfortable is the only dress requirement. A sweater draped over your shoulders will go a long way against the chill of air-conditioning. If you plan to eat in the open air, bring along insect repellent in case the mosquitoes get unruly.

We assume that restaurants and hotels accept credit cards. If they don't, we'll note it in the review.

RESERVATIONS
To ensure that you get to eat at the restaurants of your choice, make some calls or visit the website when you get to the island—especially during high season—to secure reservations. Many restaurants now have online booking options. On Sunday you may have a hard time finding a restaurant that's open for lunch; some eateries are closed all day Monday.

We mention reservations only when they're essential (there's no other way you'll ever get a table, like at intimate Chef's Table venues) or when they're not accepted. We mention dress only when men are required to wear a jacket or a jacket and tie.

Essentials

TIPPING

Most restaurants add a service charge of 15%. It's not necessary to tip once a service charge has been added to the bill, but sometimes that tip is shared between all staff. If the service is good, an additional tip of 10% is always appreciated. If no service charge is included on the final bill, then leave the customary tip of 15% to 20%.

WINES, BEER, AND SPIRITS

Arubans have a great love for wine, so even small supermarkets have a fairly good selection of European and South American wines at prices that are reasonable by Caribbean standards. The beer of choice in Aruba is the island-brewed Balashi and Balashi Chill often served with a wedge of lime, and new local brands have also surfaced like Hopi Bon and Hopi Stout. Local spirits also include *ponce crema,* a wickedly potent eggnog type of drink and *coecoei,* a thick, red-licorice-tasting liqueur that's an integral ingredient in the island's famous signature cocktail Aruba Ariba.

What It Costs in U.S. Dollars			
$	$$	$$$	$$$$
RESTAURANTS			
under $12	$12–$20	$21–$30	over $30
HOTELS			
under $275	$275–$375	$376–$475	over $475

Prices in the restaurant reviews are the average cost of a main course at dinner or, if dinner isn't served, at lunch; taxes and service charges are generally included. Prices in the hotel reviews are the lowest cost of a standard double room in high season, excluding taxes, service charges, and meal plans (except at all-inclusives). Prices for rentals are the lowest per-night cost for a one-bedroom unit in high season.

🇺🇸 Embassy/Consulate

There is no U.S. embassy on Aruba. If you need assistance you must call the embassy in Curaçao.

➕ Health and Safety

Arubans are very friendly, so you needn't be afraid to stop and ask anyone for directions. It's a relatively safe island, but commonsense rules still apply. Lock your rental car when you leave it, and leave valuables in your hotel safe. Don't leave bags unattended in the airport, on the beach, or on tour vehicles.

As a rule, water is pure and food is wholesome in hotels and local restaurants throughout Aruba, but be cautious when buying food from street vendors. And just as you would at home, wash or peel all fruits and vegetables before eating them. Traveler's diarrhea, caused by consuming contaminated water, unpasteurized milk and milk products, and unrefrigerated food, isn't a big problem—unless it happens to you. So watch what you eat, especially at outdoor buffets in the hot sun. Make sure cooked food is hot and cold food has been properly refrigerated.

The major health risk is sunburn or sunstroke. A long-sleeve shirt, a hat, and long pants or a beach wrap are essential on a boat, for midday at the beach, and whenever you go out sightseeing. Use sunscreen with an SPF of at least 15—especially if you're fair—and apply it liberally on your nose, ears, and other sensitive and exposed areas. Make sure the sunscreen is water-resistant if you're engaging in water sports. Always limit your sun time for the first few days, and drink plenty of

liquids. Limit intake of caffeine and alcohol, which hasten dehydration.

Mosquitoes can be bothersome if you are dining outside so pack (or buy on island) strong repellent (the ones that contain DEET or picaridin are the most effective). The strong trade winds generally keep them at bay during the day unless you are in thick foliage or mangrove areas near the water. It's at dusk that they come out, when winds calm, and at night when you are dining with toes in the sand. Zika and dengue have been reported on Aruba, but the island is not considered a high-risk zone. Protect yourself regardless.

Don't fly within 24 hours of scuba diving. In an emergency, Air Ambulance service will fly you to Curaçao at a low altitude if you need to get to a decompression chamber.

IMMUNIZATIONS
No special vaccinations are required to visit Aruba.

OVER-THE-COUNTER REMEDIES
There are a number of pharmacies and stores selling medications throughout the island (including at most hotels), and virtually anything obtainable in North America is available in Aruba. There is also a walk-in

Essentials

doctor's clinic at Botica di Servicio on the Palm Beach strip.

RESTROOMS

Outside Oranjestad, the public restrooms can be found in small restaurants that dot the countryside.

 Internet

Resortwide free Wi-Fi is common in Aruba. Nevertheless, some larger Aruba resort hotels offer it only in lobbies and on a few desktop computers in a business center and then charge daily rates for access in your room and other parts of the property. Many bars and dining spots and even stores now offer free Wi-Fi; just ask them for their password when you order or buy something. There are also free government-sponsored Wi-Fi hot spots and zones for tourists and locals with more to come.

 Lodging

Aruba is known for its large, luxurious high-rise resorts and vast array of time-shares. But the island also has a nice selection of smaller, low-rise resorts for travelers who don't want to feel lost in a large, impersonal hotel complex. If you're on a budget, consider booking one of the island's many apartment-style units, so you can eat in sometimes instead of having to rely on restaurants exclusively. Aruba also has Airbnb now, too.

Most Aruba hotels are found in two clusters: the low-rise hotels in a stretch along Druif Beach and Eagle Beach, and the high-rise hotels on a stretch of Palm Beach. With a few exceptions, the hotels in the high-rise area tend to be larger and more expensive than their low-rise counterparts, but they usually offer a wider range of services.

Accommodations in Aruba run the gamut from large high-rise hotels and resorts to sprawling condo complexes to small, locally owned boutique establishments, and even luxury villa rentals in well-designed private communities where fractional ownership is also an option. Most hotels are west of Oranjestad, along L. G. Smith and J. E. Irausquin Boulevards. Many are self-contained complexes, with restaurants, shops, casinos, water-sport centers, health clubs, and spas. And there are a surprising number of small and economical apartment-style hotels, bed-and-breakfasts, and family-run escapes in the interior if you know where to look. The number of all-inclusive options is growing, and increasingly, big-name-brand hotels are beginning to offer more comprehensive meal plan options. Savaneta now offers South Pacific over-the-water-style bungalows at Aruba Ocean Villas, as well as tree-house stays. Time-shares have always been big on this island, and the Divi family of resorts offers many different options in their various locations.

Large Resorts: These all-encompassing vacation destinations offer myriad dining options, casinos, shops, water-sports centers, health clubs, and car-rental desks. The island also has many all-inclusive options.

Time-Shares: Large time-share properties are also popular, luring visitors who prefer to prepare some of their own meals and have a bit more living space than you might find in the typical resort hotel room plus fully stocked kitchens with everything you need for cooking … except the food. You can order your groceries online to be stocked ahead at many resorts now, too.

Boutique Resorts: You'll find a few small resorts that offer more personal service, and better reflect the natural sense of Aruban hospitality you'll find all over the island. There are some lovely B&Bs as well.

■ TIP → **Hotels have private bathrooms, phones, and TVs, and don't offer meals unless we specify a meal plan in the review (i.e., breakfast, some meals, all meals, all-inclusive). We always list facilities but not whether you'll be charged an extra fee to use them.**

APARTMENT AND HOUSE RENTALS

Apartments and time-share condos are common in Aruba. So if you're looking for more space for your family or group to spread out in (and especially if you want to have access to a kitchen to make some meals), this can be a very budget-friendly option. The money you save can be used for more dining and activities. Many time-share resorts are full service, offering the same range of water sports and other activities as any other resort, and almost all of them offer unused units on their websites (some through third-party booking sites). And some regular resorts also have a time-share component. Airbnb (⊕ www.airbnb.com) also offers rental options on the island ranging from tiny cottage-style stays to luxurious stand-alone villas.

RESERVATIONS

When making reservations, be sure you understand how much you are really paying

Essentials

before finalizing any reservation. Hotels collect 9.5% in taxes (2% of which goes to marketing to tourists) on top of a typical 11% service charge, for a total of 20.5%. An additional $3 Environmental Levy per day was added in 2013.

Some resorts will allow you to cancel without any kind of penalty—even if you prepaid to secure a discounted rate—if you cancel at least 24 hours in advance. Others require you to cancel a week in advance or penalize you the cost of one night. Small inns and bed-and-breakfasts are most likely to require you to cancel far in advance. Most hotels allow children under a certain age to stay in their parents' room at no extra charge, but others charge for them as extra adults; find out the cutoff age for discounts.

Money

Arubans happily accept U.S. dollars virtually everywhere, so most travelers will find no real need to exchange money. The official currency is the Aruban florin (Afl), also called the guilder, which is made up of 100 cents. Silver coins come in denominations of 1, 2½, 5, 10, 25, and 50 (the square one) cents. Paper currency comes in denominations of 5, 10, 25, 50, and 100 florins.

Prices quoted throughout this book are in U.S. dollars unless otherwise noted.

For purchases you'll pay a 1.5% BBO tax (a turnover tax on each level of sale for all goods and services) in all but the duty-free shops.

Prices throughout this guide are given for adults. Substantially reduced fees are almost always available for children, students, and seniors.

ATMS AND BANKS
If you need fast cash, you'll find ATMs that accept international cards (and dispense cash in both U.S. and local currency) at banks in Oranjestad, at the major malls, and along the roads leading to the hotel strip, as well as in every casino and at the airport.

Nightlife

Aruba comes alive by night, and has become a true party hot spot. The casinos—though not as elaborate as those in Las Vegas—are among the best of any Caribbean island.

For information on specific events, check out the free magazines and their respective websites *Aruba Nights, Island*

Gourmet, Destination Aruba, and *Island Temptations,* all available at the airport and at hotels.

📦 Packing

Dress on Aruba is generally casual. Bring loose-fitting clothing made of natural fabrics to see you through days of heat and humidity. Pack a beach cover-up, both to protect yourself from the sun and to provide something to wear to and from your hotel room. Bathing suits and immodest attire are frowned upon away from the beach. A sun hat is advisable, but you don't have to pack one—inexpensive straw hats are available everywhere—but be forewarned that the wind is constant so you might have to tie it or find a firm fitting one. For shopping and sightseeing, bring shorts, jeans, T-shirts, cotton shirts, slacks, sundresses, and good walking shoes. Nighttime dress can range from very informal to casually elegant, depending on the establishment. A tie is practically never required, but a jacket may be appropriate in fancy restaurants. You may need a light sweater or jacket for evening especially when dining indoors as the air-conditioning can be set very high in many restaurants.

🎭 Performing Arts

Aruba has a handful of not-so-famous but very talented performers. Over the years, several local artists, including composer Julio Renado Euson, choreographer Wilma Kuiperi, sculptor Ciro Abath, and visual artist Elvis Lopez, have gained international renown. Furthermore, many Aruban musicians play more than one type of music (classical, jazz, soca, salsa, reggae, calypso, rap, pop), and many compose as well as perform. Edjean Semeleer has followed in the footsteps of his mentor Padu Lampe—the composer of the island's national anthem and a beloved local star—to become one of the island's best-loved entertainers. His performances pack Aruba's biggest halls, especially his annual Christmas concert. He sings in many languages, and though he's young, his style is old-style crooner—Aruba's answer to Michael Bublé. The past few years have seen a new crop of young rap and hip-hop artists also out to make their mark as well.

Essentials

Phones

To call Aruba direct from the United States, dial 011–297, followed by the seven-digit number in Aruba.

LOCAL CALLS
Dial the seven-digit number.

CALLING THE UNITED STATES
Dial 0, then 1, the area code, and the number. AT&T customers can dial 800–8000 from special phones at the cruise dock and in the airport's arrival and departure halls and charge calls to their credit card.

MOBILE PHONES
Both SETAR and Digicel offer rental phones, but if you are staying for more than a week, it may be just as cost-effective to buy a cheap phone; even easier is buying a prepaid local SIM and using it in your own unlocked phone. Most U.S.–based GSM and CDMA cell phones work on Aruba.

If you have a multiband phone (some countries use frequencies different from those used in the United States) and your service provider uses the world-standard GSM network (as do T-Mobile, AT&T, and Verizon), you can probably use your phone abroad. Roaming fees can be steep. And overseas you normally pay the toll charges for incoming calls. It's almost always cheaper to send a text message than to make a call.

■TIP→ **Take advantage of the island's abundant free Wi-Fi and use Internet-based apps for making calls like Google Hangouts and WhatsApp.**

Shipping

Post Aruba's website has all the information you need for sending mail. From Aruba to the United States or Canada a letter costs Afl2.20 (about $1.25) and a postcard costs Afl1.30 (75¢). Expect it to take one to two weeks. When addressing letters to Aruba, don't worry about the lack of formal addresses or postal codes; the island's postal service knows where to go.

If you need to send a package in a hurry, there are a few options. FedEx offers overnight service to the United States if you get your package in before 3 pm; there is a convenient office in downtown Oranjestad. Another big courier service is UPS, and several smaller local courier services, most of them open weekdays 9 to 5, also provide international deliveries.

🛍 Shopping

Shopping can be good on Aruba. Although stores on the island often use the tagline "duty-free," the word "prices" is usually printed underneath in much smaller letters. The only real duty-free shopping is in the departures area of the airport. (Passengers bound for the United States should be sure to shop before proceeding through U.S. customs in Aruba.) Downtown stores do have very low sales tax, though, and they offer some excellent bargains on high-end luxury items like gold, silver, gems, and high-end watches. Major credit cards are welcome everywhere, as are U.S. dollars.

A good way to preview the shops and malls in downtown Oranjestad is to hop aboard the free trolley that loops the downtown area. There are some interesting new offerings in the backstreets, including big name-brand megastores wedged in between smaller mom-and-pop shops. Also the smaller malls along the strip like the Village Square have some unique artisan shops, as does Paseo Herencia, whose courtyard is the scene of nightly entertainment called "the Waltzing Waters."

Aruba's souvenir and crafts stores are full of delft Dutch porcelains and figurines, as befits the island's heritage. Dutch cheese is a good buy, as are hand-embroidered linens and any products made from the native aloe vera plant—sunburn cream, face masks, or skin refreshers found in the many official Aruba Aloe stores; new eco-friendly sunscreen mandated by law is also available. Local arts and crafts run toward wood carvings and earthenware emblazoned with "Aruba: One Happy Island" and the like, but there are many shops with unique Aruban items like designer wear and fancy flip-flops and artwork if you know where to look. And arts foundations like Cosecha in Oranjestad and San Nicolas offer up only certifiably authentic, high-quality arts and crafts made in Aruba by talented local artisans. Don't try to bargain unless you are at a flea market or stall. Arubans consider it rude to haggle, despite what you may hear to the contrary.

There is late-night shopping in two locations. The first, in downtown Oranjestad at Renaissance Mall—a multilevel indoor-outdoor complex—stays open until 8 pm, and shops in the modern, multilevel indoor shopping mall off the high-rise strip—Palm Beach Plaza—stay open until 10 pm. Many of the shops around Paseo Herencia also stay open late in high

Essentials

season. A few other shops that stay open late can be found in Alhambra Mall as well. And most resorts have their own shops, but don't expect plastic bags for your goods or groceries, as Aruba banned them in 2017. There are really nice reusable bags for purchase all over the place that are made from recycled materials, and some of them are imprinted with authentic Aruba scenes that make great souvenirs as well.

📍 Visitor Information

HOLIDAYS

Aruba's official holidays are New Year's Day, Good Friday, Easter Sunday, and Christmas, as well as Betico Croes Day (January 25), National Anthem and Flag Day (March 18), King's Day (April 30), Labor Day (May 1), and Ascension Day (39 days after Easter).

WEDDINGS

People over the age of 18 can marry as long as they submit the appropriate documents 14 days in advance. Couples are required to submit birth certificates with raised seals, through the mail or in person, to Aruba's Office of the Civil Registry. They also need an apostil—a document proving they're free to marry—from their country of residence.

Same-sex ceremonies are available on Aruba, though they're not legally binding.

With so many beautiful spots to choose from, weddings on Aruba are guaranteed to be romantic. Most resorts have their own wedding planning department or use a local partner and they can handle everything from start to finish for you. Aruba also now hosts the world's largest vow renewal group ceremony for couples from all over the world on Eagle Beach each year.

📅 When to Go

Aruba's high season runs from early December through mid-April. During this season you're guaranteed the most entertainment at resorts and the most people with whom to enjoy it. January and February are the most expensive times to visit, both for people staying a week or more and for cruise-ship passengers coming ashore. During this period hotels are solidly booked, and you must make reservations at least two or three months in advance for the very best places (and to get the best airfares). During the rest of the year hotel prices can drop 20% to 40% after April 15.

Contacts

Air

CONTACTS Air Transat. ☎ 877/872–6728 ⊕ www.air-transat.com. **Sunwing Airlines.** ☎ 800/877–1755 ⊕ www.sun-wing.ca. **Westjet.** ☎ 888/937–8538 ⊕ www.westjet.com.

Bicycle

CONTACTS Aruba E-Bike Tours. ☎ 297/592–5550 ⊕ www.arubaebiketours.com. **Aruba Motorcycle Tours.** ☎ 297/641–7818 ⊕ arubamotorcycletours.com. **Green Bike Aruba.** ☎ 297/594–6368 ⊕ greenbikearuba.com.

Bus

CONTACTS Arubus. ⊕ www.arubus.com.

Car

CAR RENTALS Amigo. ☎ 297/583–8833 ⊕ www.amigocar.com. **Avis.** ☎ 297/582–5496 in Aruba, 800/532–1527 ⊕ www.avis.com. **Budget.** ☎ 297/582–8600, 800/472–3325 in Aruba ⊕ www.budgetaruba.com. **Thrifty.** ☎ 297/583–4902 ⊕ www.thriftycarrentalaruba.com. **Tropic Car Rental.**

☎ 297/583–7336 ⊕ www.tropiccarrent-aruba.com.

PARKING Aruparking. ⊕ www.aruparking.com.

 Embassy/Consulate

CONTACTS U.S. Consulate Curaçao. ⊠ J.B. Gorsiraweg 1, Willemstad ☎ 9/461–3066 ⊕ cw.usconsulate.gov.

Phones

CONTACTS Digicel. ☎ 297/522–2222 ⊕ www.digicelaruba.com. **SETAR.** ☎ 297/525–1000 ⊕ www.setar.aw.

🚕 Taxi

CONTACTS Arubas Transfer Tour & Taxi C.A.. ⊠ Airport ☎ 297/582–2116, 297/582–2010 ⊕ www.airportaruba.com/taxi-transportation.

📍 Visitor Information

CONTACTS Aruba Food and Beverage Association. ☎ 297/280–1312 ⊕ www.arubadining.com. **Aruba Hotel & Tourism Association.** ☎ 297/582–2607 ⊕ www.ahata.com. **Aruba Tourism Authority.** ⊠ L. G. Smith Blvd. 8, Oranjestad ☎ 800/862–7822 in

Contacts

the U.S./international, 297/582–3777 in Aruba ⊕ *www.aruba.com.* **Papiamento Online Courses.** ⊕ *cudoo.com.* **Post Aruba.** ⊕ *www.postaruba.com.*

WEDDINGS Aruba Fairy Tales Weddings. ⊠ *Costa Linda Beach Resort* ☎ *297/593–0045,* ⊕ *arubafairytales.com.* **Aruba Weddings for You.** ☎ *297/525–5293* ⊕ *www.arubaweddings-foryou.com.* **Dream Weddings Aruba.** ⊠ *Matadera 9W, Noord* ☎ *297/587–5991* ⊕ *www.dreamweddingsaruba.com.*

Papiamento Primer

Papiamento is a hybrid language born out of the colorful past of Aruba, Bonaire, and Curaçao. The language's use is generally thought to have started in the 17th century when Sephardic Jews migrated with their African slaves from Brazil to Curaçao. The slaves spoke a pidgin Portuguese, which may have been blended with pure Portuguese, some Dutch (the colonial power in charge of the island), and Arawakan. Proximity to the mainland meant that Spanish and English words were also incorporated.

Papiamento is roughly translated as "the way of speaking." (Sometimes the suffix -mentu is spelled in the Spanish and Portuguese way [-mento], creating the variant spelling.) It began as an oral tradition, handed down through the generations and spoken by all social classes on the islands. There's no uniform spelling or grammar from island to island, or even from one neighborhood to another. Nevertheless, it's beginning to receive some official recognition, and anyone applying for citizenship must be fluent in both Papiamento and Dutch.

Arubans enjoy it when visitors use their language, so don't be shy. You can buy a Papiamento dictionary to build your vocabulary, and there are online courses and videos to help you as well, but here are a few pleasantries to get you started:

Bon dia. Good morning.

Bon tardi. Good afternoon.

Bon nochi. Good evening/night.

Bon bini. Welcome.

Ayo. Bye.

Te aworo. See you later.

Pasa un bon dia. Have a good day.

Danki. Thank you.

Na bo ordo. You're welcome.

Con ta bai? How are you?

Mi ta bon. I am fine.

Ban goza! Let's enjoy!

Pabien! Congratulations!

Quanto costa esaki? How much is this?

Hopi bon. Very good.

Ami. Me.

Abo. You.

Nos dos. The two of us.

Mi dushi. My sweetheart.

Dushi. Sweet or cool.

Ku tur mi amor. With all my love.

Un braza. A hug.

Un sunchi. A kiss.

Mi stima Aruba. I love Aruba.

How to Spend 5 Days in Aruba

If you're heading to One Happy Island, you probably intend to spend a lot at time on the beach, but there are some excellent reasons to roll out of that surf-side hammock and explore more of Aruba, some of which include some quality time in the sea. But don't worry, all of Aruba's beaches are public, so you can take a dip wherever you like.

DAY 1: PALM BEACH PLEASURES

Even if you're staying elsewhere, **Palm Beach** is worth a visit on your first day to see where all the action is. Make sure you come in your bathing suit (with a change of clothes) because this area is famous for its water sports and sailing and snorkel excursions, as well as its dining, shopping, and nightlife options. It's safe to walk day or night, and compact enough to discover on foot. Visit the **Butterfly Farm Aruba** while there: the visit takes about an hour or so, and your initial admission is good for repeat visits ... just in case. Plan for lunch at one of the many beachfront cafés, take-outs, or pier bars.

After dark, don't miss the colorful free nightly water shows at **Paseo Herencia**—this is also where most of the glitzy casinos are located. If you end your day at Paseo Herencia,

head to **Melt Away Cafe** for dinner. If you decide to hit up the **Casino Aruba** at the Hilton, plan for dinner at the **Sunset Grille.** If you're heading north on the strip towards the **Aruba Marriott Resort** or its **Stellaris Casino,** dinner at **Atardi** is a good bet, especially if you're looking for toes-in-the-sand dining.

LOGISTICS

Accessible by public bus or taxi, or simply drive along Route 1B, which runs along the coast from tip to tip. (1A is northbound, 1B is southbound.)

DAY 2: DOWNTOWN DELIGHTS

You'll spend an entire day discovering downtown **Oranjestad's** colorful mélange of local eateries, shops, historic buildings, and newly refurbished main streets. It's an easily walkable grid, but if you don't feel like walking, you can hop on and off the free **Downtown Trolley,** or join a guided outing with **Aruba Walking Tours.** If you're hot after shopping, head to the urban oasis known as **Surfside Beach** less than a mile away to cool off. Enjoy a stellar sunset there, and perhaps a cocktail and snack at **Surfside Beach Bar,** then head to the lively marina of **Renaissance Marketplace** for casinos, alfresco dining, nightlife, and free live entertainment.

LOGISTICS

Take Route 1B straight to downtown, take a taxi, or hop a public bus.

DAY 3: GO WILD

Today's the day to explore **Arikok National Park,** the island's wild and untamed arid outback, with a guided UTV, ATV, or jeep safari with an operator like **De Palm Tours.** Don't miss the surreal thrill of swimming or snorkeling in the **Conchi,** a remote natural pool, or exploring the **Fontein Cave,** which has the island's only Arawak Indians drawings. Most tours leave on the early side, so plan to grab a quick breakfast at the hotel. If you choose a full-day affair, lunch will be included, but plan dinner at your resort as you'll be exhausted after the tour and won't want to venture far. If you choose to do a half-day tour, do so in the morning so you can head back to your resort afterward to have some time at the hotel's pool or at the beach before having dinner at the hotel. You'll need the downtime, trust us.

LOGISTICS

You can drive there, but it's not recommended for first-timers. All tours include hotel pick-up and drop off, so sit back and let the adventure begin.

DAY 4: SLEUTH OUT SOUTHEAST COAST SURPRISES

Rent a car and head southeast to discover the best locally caught fish and seafood meals at **Zeerovers** for lunch in **Savaneta,** and then head back to Route 1 to continue on to **San Nicolas** to see why it's called Aruba's answer to Miami's Wynwood area. The outdoor art is epic. If you want to know more about the art, join a jaunt with **Aruba Murals Tours.** Just don't forget your bathing suit, because you'll want to head on to **Baby Beach** for a dip and an hour or two of beach time. Head back to Savaneta for dinner at **Flying Fishbone.** ■ TIP→ **Reserve ahead at Flying Fishbone if you want to dine with your feet in the water.**

LOGISTICS

For San Nicolas, follow Route 1A, for Savaneta, make a right turn at the Super S-Chows' Supermarket, follow the sign for Flying Fishbone. Get back on 1A for San Nicolas.

DAY 5: YOUR LAST DAY

Flights usually leave in the late afternoon; spend an hour or so at the beach before heading to the airport. Make sure to leave plenty of time at the airport, as there are about seven steps that involve picking up and dropping your luggage numerous times before you

How to Spend 5 Days in Aruba

clear Customs and can head to the waiting areas. Once there, have a last tropical cocktail in **The Crying Room,** a small corner of the airport's One Happy Bar, aptly named as it's famous for inducing the tears of those who always hate to leave Aruba.

WHAT HAPPENS IF IT RAINS?

Even though Aruba is outside the hurricane belt, you may find yourself with the rare rainy day, or you might just want a break from the tropical heat if you overdid the sunbathing. That's a perfect time to explore some of the museums and the art gallery in downtown Oranjestad and ride the free eco-trolley around the newly refreshed Main Street and see what's on offer. There are lots of souvenir and high-end shopping options there, or you can head to modern, multilevel Palm Beach Plaza for all kinds of shopping, entertainment, and movies. They also have a food court and several lunch options in the immediate vicinity. You can also enjoy some first-rate pampering at one of the island's many premium spas—maybe an aloe-based treatment to soothe your overly sunned skin? This island has some of the world's best-quality aloe products. Or how about a couple's massage by

the sea under a tiki hut? If you want more action, the casinos are always ready to receive you. Some are open 24 hours a day, and sometimes they offer daytime bingo as well, for something different to do.

Best Tours

Tours

You can see the main sights in one day, but set aside two days to really meander. Guided tours are your best option if you have only a short time.

TOUR OPERATORS

There are many first-rate tour operators on Aruba, and the adventures range from wild and crazy jeep safaris in the outback to Segway tours along the coast to sea and sand discovery and even historical, art, and foodie walking tours. A good way to get your bearings is to take a bus tour around the island's main highlights—it's a small island so it will not take more than half a day—with a well-established company like De Palm Tours.

★ Aruba Walking Tours

LOCAL INTEREST | Explore the heartbeat of *One Happy Island* and learn all about its fascinating history on the Aruba Historic Cultural Downtown Walking Tour, which lasts about 2½ hours and covers about 30 stops including a cooking demonstration. They also offer a foodie adventure at night called Fusions of World Food Tour that stops at five places that have intrinsic ties. Complimentary pickup is included from most hotels (but not drop-off), and private and custom tours are also available.

■ TIP → **The big metal solar tree sculpture at the meeting spot has smartphone charging outlets within it.** ✉ *Zoutmanstraat 1, Oranjestad* ☎ *297/699–0995* ⊕ *www.arubawalkingtours.com* 🎫 *$39* ⊗ *No tours Sun.*

BIKE TOURS

Guided bike tours are offered with Green Bike and Aruba BikeTours. Rancho Notorious offers mountain biking tours. Aruba Motorcycle Tours is a unique way to see the island.

★ Aruba E-Bike Tours

BICYCLING | This operator offers fat-tire electric bicycles that can give you a power boost when you need it. Visitors can choose any one of four hour-long guided tours around the island. There are daily departures in the early morning and at sunset, and points of interest include the California Lighthouse and Alto Vista Chapel. Helmets and visibility vests are included. Children must be 12 and over. ✉ *Paseo Herencia Mall, J. E. Irausquin Blvd. 328A, Palm Beach* ☎ *297/592–5550* ⊕ *www. arubaebiketours.com* 🎫 *From $45.*

Aruba Motorcycle Tours

BICYCLING | Hog fans will adore this novel way to tour Aruba. On your own Harley with a rental, or in one of their guided group tours—a four-hour trip that takes only

Best Tours

the back roads to bring you the island's best sites—you will enjoy the open road like a rebel with this outfit. A motorcycle license and $1,000 deposit is required with each tour. For rentals alone, a $2,000 deposit is required. Helmets are supplied, and pickup and drop-off at hotels is offered. All renters and group riders must be over 21. ⊠ *Jaburibari 16-C, Noord* ☎ *297/ 641–7818* ⊕ *www.arubamotorcycletours. com* 🖾 *Tours from $50 (on top of rental).*

★ Green Bike Aruba Tours

BICYCLING | The same company that supplies the grab-and-go shared bike kiosks around the island also offers two group-bike tours. One explores the beaches around the California Lighthouse and includes a stop there, and the other explores downtown and the Linear Park. Both tours include a well-informed guide, a bike cooler basket with snacks and water, and free Wi-Fi as you tour. Bring or wear your bathing suit as they take swim stops, too. ⊠ *Ponto 69, Oranjestad* ☎ *297/594–6368* ⊕ *www. greenbikearuba.com* 🖾 *From $39.*

Rancho Notorious

BICYCLE TOURS | If mountain biking is more your thing, tours are offered through the Aruban countryside on old donkey trails—there are more than 200 mountain bike trails on the island—for half or full days. Bikes are TREK aluminum mountain bikes. ⊠ *Boroncana, Noord* ☎ *297/586–0508* ⊕ *www.ranchonotorious.com.*

BOAT TOURS

Snorkeling and sunset party cruises are the norm, but some also include dinner or have dinner on shore after your voyage. Most seaborne tours depart from Palm Beach at either Pelican Pier De Palm Pier, or the Hadicurari Pier, with a few exceptions departing from downtown Oranjestad. There are also semi-submarine and submarine tours with Atlantis Submarines (operated by De Palm Tours), which operates a 65-foot air-conditioned sub that takes 48 passengers 95 to 130 feet below the surface along Barcadera Reef. The two-hour trip (including boat transfer to the submarine platform and 50-minute plunge) has garnered multiple awards for best tour and one for green operations. Make reservations one day in advance. Another option is the *Seaworld Explorer,* a semisubmersible also operated by Atlantis Submarines that allows you to view Aruba's marine habitat from 6 feet below the surface.

CONTACTS De Palm Tours. ⊠ *L. G. Smith Blvd. 142, Oranjestad*

☎ 297/582–4400, 800/766–
6016 ⊕ www.depalm.com.
Pelican Adventures. ✉ J. E.
Irausquin Blvd. 232, Oranjestad
☎ 297/587–2302 ⊕ www.
pelican-aruba.com.

FOOD TOURS
★ Fusion of the World Food Tour
WALKING TOURS | Discover five
different dining spots for tapas
and drinks—each with an
inherent connection to Aruba—
and all within walking distance
of each other in downtown
Oranjestad. This two-and-a-half-
hour foodie tour takes place
in the evening with a local
guide who will also fill you in
on some history and highlights
of the downtown attractions
and neighborhoods you are
exploring. The pace is leisurely
and complimentary pickup
and drop-off from the major
resort areas can be included.
✉ Cosecha building, Zoutmanstraat 1 ✛ Across the street
from the big yellow Cosecha
building, look for the Aruba
Walking Tours meeting point
sign ☎ 297/699–0995 ⊕ www.
arubawalkingtours.com/aruba-
food-tour 🖃 $79.

★ Kukoo Kunuku Party & Foodie Tours
SPECIAL-INTEREST | Best known
for their wild and crazy bar-
hopping tours aboard brightly
painted red party buses, this
outfit also dials it down a notch
for their foodie tours like the

Dinner & Nightlife Tour that
includes a sunset champagne
toast or the Wine On Down The
Road tour, which features an
onboard sommelier and stops
at some of Aruba's finest dining spots for wine and tapas.
They are planning to offer a
craft and local beer and bites
tour, too. ☎ 297/586–2010
⊕ www.kukookunuku.com
🖃 From $50.

SPECIALTY TOURS
Aruba's interior is rugged and
rocky and best explored with
an all-terrain vehicle, especially
if you want to explore the cacti-studded countryside or visit
the natural pool or other incredible landmarks like the small
natural bridges or the wild
coast. The island's largest tour
operators like De Palm Tours
and ABC Tours offer the most
choices when it comes to jeep
safaris and UTV tours, but if
you want to go it alone, then
it's best to rent a rough-and-
tumble vehicle from a company
that specializes in them like Off
Road Evolution Aruba.

ABC Tours
ADVENTURE TOURS | Jeep and
UTV tour itineraries include
visits to Aruba's interesting historical sites as well as natural
monuments like the natural
pool and Indian Cave. ✉ Schot-
landstraat 61, Oranjestad
☎ 297/582–5600 ⊕ abc-aruba.
com.

On the Calender

YEAR-ROUND
Bon Bini Festival. Local music and dance festival Tuesday nights at Fort Zoutman. ⊕ aruba-regatta.com

Island Festival. Monthly cultural music, dance, and food event in San Nicolas. ⊕ www.islandfestivalaruba.com

Meet San Nicolas. Monthly cultural street party.

JANUARY–MARCH
Carnival. Weeks of parties and cultural events precede this two-day street party in late February or early March. ⊕ aruba-regatta.com

MARCH
National Flag and Anthem Day. March 18th brings celebrations to the streets. ⊕ aruba-regatta.com

APRIL
King's Day. On April 27, Aruba celebrates Dutch King Willem's birthday with outdoor activities.

Eat Local's Food Truck Festival. Last week of April in downtown Oranjestad. ⊕ aruba-regatta.com

MAY
Soul Beach Music Festival. Memorial Day Weekend event attracts famous international music talents. ⊕ www.soulbeach.net

JUNE
KLM Aruba Marathon. Marathon day also includes a half marathon, a 10K, and a 5K. ⊕ arubainternationalmarathon.com

JULY
Aruba Hi-Winds. An annual massive windsurfing and kiteboarding competition with parties. ⊕ hiwindsaruba.com

AUGUST
Aruba I Do. On August 22, hundreds of couples renew vows on Eagle Beach. ⊕ aruba-regatta.com

Aruba International Regatta. Three days of great boat races and parties in mid-August. ⊕ aruba-regatta.com

OCTOBER
Eat Local Restaurant Month. The month of October offers local dining specials and events. ⊕ aruba-regatta.com

Island TakeOver Festival. 4-day music festival with local and international artists. ⊕ islandtakeover.com

NOVEMBER
Aruba Art Fair. San Nicolas invites international artists to permanently beautify sunrise city. ⊕ aruba-regatta.com

Aruba Open Beach Tennis Championships. A massive international tennis competition the second week of November with parties. ⊕ arubabeachtennisopen.com

DECEMBER
Dande Festival. Local musicians welcome the new year with original songs and competitions. ⊕ aruba-regatta.com

ORANJESTAD

Updated by
Sue Campbell

⊙ Sights	🍴 Restaurants	🛏 Hotels	🛍 Shopping	🍸 Nightlife
★★★☆☆	★★★★☆	★★☆☆☆	★★★★☆	★★★★☆

NEIGHBORHOOD SNAPSHOT

TOP EXPERIENCES

■ **Shop for Luxury:** Shop Downtown's upscale shops for gold, silver, timepieces, and brand-name fashions.

■ **Try Your Luck:** Stop into one of the glitzy world-class casinos to cool off and seduce lady luck.

■ **Walking Tours:** Explore downtown Oranjestad's culture, history, and food with Aruba Walking Tours.

■ **Trolley Tour:** Hop on the free trolley to preview the eclectic maze of superb shopping and dining options.

■ **Surfside Beach:** Grab a green bike and head out on the paved seaside trail to discover this lovely little urban beach.

GETTING HERE AND AROUND

Oranjestad is accessible by car, taxi, or bus. It's about 15 minutes from the airport to the downtown core, and if you're staying in the low-rise or high-rise region of the island, you'll drive right down the main thoroughfare. Coming to town from Eagle Beach is about a 10-minute drive, and from Palm Beach about 20–25 minutes depending on your location and traffic.

Public buses run frequently and stop at just about every major resort along the way, stopping at the downtown terminal steps and all the best attractions. Taxis are easy to get for your way back if you're staying out late.

The pedestrian-only walkway and resting areas have made Aruba's capital very walkable. The Downtown Trolley is free and a great way to get around, too.

QUICK BITES

■ **The Pastechi House.** Look for the big smiling pastechi sign and a line of locals waiting to grab Aruba's favorite fast food (think empanada), and wash it down with a cold *batido* (fruit shake). ⊠ *Caya G. F. Betico Croes 42, Oranjestad* Ⓜ *Downtown Trolley line*

■ **Coffee Break.** The island's only locally roasted coffee is only available here. They also offer gelato, pastries, and sandwiches. ⊠ *Caya G.F. Betico Croes 101-A, Oranjestad* ⊕ *arubacoffeeroasters.com* Ⓜ *Downtown Trolley line*

■ **Gelatissmobistro.** Enjoy homemade gelato and a wide range of snacks and drinks at this alfresco bar. ⊠ *Emmastraat 1 (across from Zara and behind Renaissance Mall)* ⊕ *www.giannisgroup.com* Ⓜ *Downtown Trolley line*

Aruba's historic port capital city Oranjestad has always had a colorful Dutch colonial charm, but the past few years have seen a major face-lift and renewal throughout downtown to better accommodate a growing local population and better welcome the 2 million-plus visitors it sees each year.

Aruba's capital is easily explored on foot. Its palm-lined central thoroughfare runs between old and new pastel-painted buildings of typical Dutch design (Spanish influence is also evident in some of the architecture), and new walking tours help you discover its history, culture, and food. There are a lot of malls with boutiques and shops—the Renaissance Mall carries high-end luxury items and designer fashions. A massive renovation has given Main Street (aka Caya G. F. Betico Croes) behind the Renaissance Marina Resort a whole new lease on life: boutique malls, shops, and restaurants have opened next to well-loved family-run businesses. The pedestrian-only walkway and resting areas have unclogged the streets, and the eco-trolley is free and a great way to get around if you don't want to walk—you can hop on and hop off when you like. The Linear Park (an ongoing project that will connect downtown to the main tourist beaches by boardwalk) begins in Oranjestad and runs all the way to the airport, providing locals and visitors alike with a scenic paved path along the sea to walk, bike, or jog, and also use the free public fitness equipment along the way; when completed it will be the longest park of its kind in the Caribbean. And the newly popular urban Surfside Beach is where you can partake in upscale seaside lounging, funky beach bars, and a massive floating water park full of fun for the family, just minutes from the downtown core.

Sights

Aruba Aloe Museum & Factory

FARM/RANCH | Aruba has the ideal conditions to grow the aloe vera plant. It's an important export, and there are aloe stores all over the island. The museum and factory tour reveal the process of extracting the serum to make many products used for beauty, health, and healing. Guided or self-guided tours are available

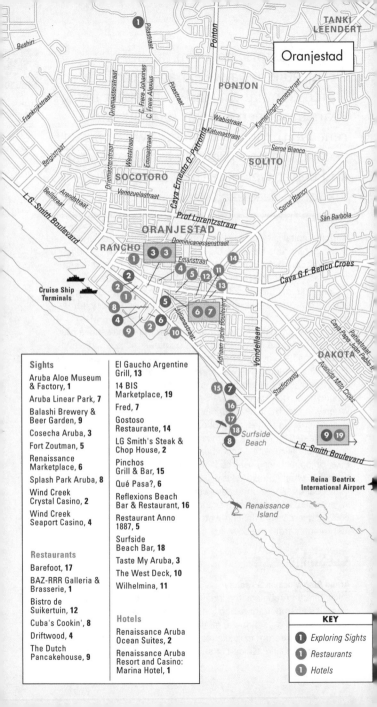

Oranjestad

TANKI LEENDERT

PONTON

SOLITO

SOCOTORO

ORANJESTAD

RANCHO

Cruise Ship Terminals

DAKOTA

Surfside Beach

Reina Beatrix International Airport

Renaissance Island

Sights

Aruba Aloe Museum & Factory, **1**

Aruba Linear Park, **7**

Balashi Brewery & Beer Garden, **9**

Cosecha Aruba, **3**

Fort Zoutman, **5**

Renaissance Marketplace, **6**

Splash Park Aruba, **8**

Wind Creek Crystal Casino, **2**

Wind Creek Seaport Casino, **4**

Restaurants

Barefoot, **17**

BAZ-RRR Galleria & Brasserie, **1**

Bistro de Suikertuin, **12**

Cuba's Cookin', **8**

Driftwood, **4**

The Dutch Pancakehouse, **9**

El Gaucho Argentine Grill, **13**

14 BIS Marketplace, **19**

Fred, **7**

Gostoso Restaurante, **14**

LG Smith's Steak & Chop House, **2**

Pinchos Grill & Bar, **15**

Qué Pasa?, **6**

Reflexions Beach Bar & Restaurant, **16**

Restaurant Anno 1887, **5**

Surfside Beach Bar, **18**

Taste My Aruba, **3**

The West Deck, **10**

Wilhelmina, **11**

Hotels

Renaissance Aruba Ocean Suites, **2**

Renaissance Aruba Resort and Casino: Marina Hotel, **1**

KEY

1 Exploring Sights

1 Restaurants

1 Hotels

in English, Dutch, Spanish, and Papiamento. There's a store to purchase their products on-site, and they are also available online. ⊠ *Pitastraat 115, Oranjestad* ☎ *800/952–7822* ⊕ *www.arubaaloe. com* 🎫 *Free.*

★ Aruba Linear Park

CITY PARK | FAMILY | Plaza Turismo, off Surfside Beach, is the anchor of the Linear Park which, when completed, will connect both main tourist beaches along the coast by boardwalks and walking paths. The first leg—a smooth paved biking and jogging trail that runs from downtown Oranjestad along the sea all the way to the airport—is complete. There are many cafés, bars, and snack stops along the way, and there are also fitness pit stops with free-to-use public fitness equipment. It's a popular stretch for local fun runs and fitness initiatives, and locals and visitors use the easy-to-access Green Bike rental kiosks. Much like "Bixi Bike" operations, you can use your credit card to grab a bike and then leave it at another stop. The plaza has also become a go-to spot for cultural events and outdoor entertainment. When complete, the Linear Park will be the longest of its kind in the entire Caribbean. ⊠ *Surfside Beach, Oranjestad* ⊕ *www.facebook.com/pages/Linear-Park-Aruba/295830233779416* 🎫 *Free.*

Balashi Brewery & Beer Garden

RESTAURANT—SIGHT | Aruba is the only nation in the world to make beer out of desalinated seawater, and it's really good beer! They also make a version called Chill with added lemon flavor and new upscale brews called Hopi Bon ("very good" in Papiamento) and Hopi Stout (good stout). See how it's all done at the factory just outside of Oranjestad proper and sample some of the beers afterward. There is also a lovely outdoor beer garden for lunch and drinks that's open until 3 pm weekdays. Closed-toe shoes are required for the factory tour, which is offered Monday through Thursday from 9 am to noon. ⊠ *Balashi 62, Balashi* ☎ *297/585–8700* ⊕ *www.balashibrewery.com* 🎫 *$10, includes one free beer* ⊘ *Closed weekends. No tours Fri.*

★ Cosecha Aruba

MUSEUM | One of the many historic buildings repurposed as an attraction over the past few years, this arts foundation displays only the works of local artisans. The building houses workshops, a gallery, and a design shop where visitors can purchase exquisite souvenirs. All artisans selling and showing wares here must be "Seyo" certified, a national seal that ensures that all work is locally made, of excellent quality, and reflects Aruban heritage. The beautifully restored 100-year-old mansion in which it's located is worth a visit on its own. There's another Cosecha in San Nicolas

Brewing Up Something Special

Order a "Balashi cocktail" in Aruba only if you want to receive a glass of water. That's because the water purification plant is in Balashi. And don't be afraid to drink the water: it's safe and delicious and made from desalinated seawater. But since the advent of the beer called Balashi—the only beer in the world made from desalinated seawater—you might confuse a barkeep if you order just a "Balashi." The brewery has regularly scheduled tours should you want to see how it's made, and they also have a great beer garden and lunch spot. Try a Balashi Chill with a wedge of lime in the neck, like many Mexican beers. Hopi Bon ("very good" in Papiamento) and Hopi Stout ("good stout") are the latest beer brews.

with art workshops for visitors. ⊠ *Zoutmanstraat 1, Oranjestad* ☎ *297/578–8709* ⊕ *www.arubacosecha.com* ⊙ *Closed Sun.*

Fort Zoutman

MILITARY SITE | One of the island's oldest edifices, Aruba's historic fort was built in 1796 and played an important role in skirmishes between British and Curaçao troops in 1803. The Willem III Tower, named for the Dutch monarch of that time, was added in 1868 to serve as a lighthouse. Over time the fort has been a government office building, a police station, and a prison; now its historical museum displays Aruban artifacts in an 18th-century house. This is also the site of the weekly Tuesday-night welcome party called the Bon Bini festival, with local music, food, and dance. If you visit with Aruba Walking Tours you can climb to the roof for great views. ⊠ *Zoutmanstraat, Oranjestad* ☎ *297/588–5199* 🎫 *$5* ⊙ *Closed Sun.*

Renaissance Marketplace

ARTS VENUE | **FAMILY** | The complex beside the Oranjestad marina and the park around it is the place where you're most likely to happen upon some great free entertainment, including pop-up festivals. Although there's live entertainment every night at the far end in the common area bandstand, most of the bars and cafés also invite their own bands. You'll also find a casino, movie theaters, and arty little shops that are open late. Occasionally, there's a local farmers' market or a big gala music festival going on. Even if there's no planned additional activity, it's a wonderful spot to explore in the evening to experience a truly enchanting and electrical tropical night full of colorful lights and sounds along the water.

Built in 1798 by the Dutch army, Fort Zoutman is Aruba's oldest structure.

✉ *9 Loyd G. Smith Blvd., Oranjestad* ⊕ *www.renaissancearubaresortandcasino.com* ▦ *Free.*

Splash Park Aruba

AMUSEMENT PARK/WATER PARK | **FAMILY** | Few people realize that you can swim in downtown Oranjestad at Surfside Beach just off the new Linear Park. And now families can enjoy a unique attraction there as well. Splash Park Aruba is a huge inflatable maze of obstacles, jungle gyms, swings, slides, and climbing towers. It's a great way to cool off after downtown shopping and sightseeing with lots of aqua fun for the whole family (children six and over only). They will also pick you up from your hotel for morning or afternoon packages. ✉ *Surfside Beach, Oranjestad* ☎ *297/594–1002* ⊕ *www.splashparkaruba.com* ▦ *$15 (admission for 1 hr only); $30 (admission plus hotel pickup).*

CASINOS

Wind Creek Crystal Casino

CASINO—SIGHT | Adorned with Austrian crystal chandeliers and gold-leaf columns, the Renaissance Aruba's glittering casino evokes Monaco's grand establishments. The Salon Privé offers serious gamblers a private room for baccarat, roulette, and high-stakes blackjack. This casino is popular among cruise-ship passengers, who stroll over from the port to watch and play in slot tournaments and bet on sporting events. Luxury car giveaways are also a big draw there. It's open 24 hours and there's live entertainment Tuesday through Sunday. ✉ *Renaissance Aruba Resort*

& Casino, L. G. Smith Blvd. 82, Oranjestad ☎ 297/583–6000 ⊕ www.windcreekaruba.com.

★ Wind Creek Seaport Casino

CASINO—SIGHT | A super-lively and fun casino right on the waterfront and across the street from the lively Renaissance Marketplace, this place has more than 300 modern slots as well as four blackjack tables, Caribbean stud, roulette, regular poker, Texas hold 'em, and daily bingo starting at noon. They also have state-of-the-art race and sports book operations. It's open until 4 am. ⊠ L. G. Smith Blvd. 9, Oranjestad ☎ 297/583–6000 ext. 6318 ⊕ www.windcreekaruba.com.

 Beaches

Renaissance Island

BEACH—SIGHT | **FAMILY** | This tiny tropical oasis is accessible only to guests of the Renaissance Marina and Renaissance Ocean Suite hotels unless you buy an expensive day pass, which is not always available. Free boat shuttles pick up guests in the lower lobby or from the helipad in the marina. Iguana Beach is family-friendly, while Flamingo Beach is limited to adults and hosts a flock of resident flamingos. (Children may visit the flamingos for a photo op daily from 10 to 11 am but must have an adult present.) The waters are clear and full of colorful fish; swimming is in a protected area, and there's a full-service restaurant, a beach bar, and waiter service on the beach. Rent a cabana for more luxuries. If you book a spa treatment, you can spend the rest of the day on the island for free. **Amenities:** food and drink; toilets; showers. **Best for:** swimming; water sports; snorkeling. ⊠ Oranjestad ✛ Accessible by water taxi only from the Renaissance Aruba Hotel & Marina ☎ 297/583–6000 ⊕ www.arubaprivateisland.com ☷ Day pass $125.

Surfside Beach

BEACH—SIGHT | Accessible by public bus, car, or taxi, this little beach has come back to life just outside downtown Oranjestad with beach bars, a paved path of the Linear Park passing by, and Plaza Turismo. It's also the spot of Splash Park Aruba, an inflatable water park. This is an ideal spot to stop for a dip when cycling or jogging along the bike path or strolling around the town. **Amenities:** food and drink; parking (free); toilets; water sports. **Best for:** swimming; partiers; sunsets. ⊠ L. G. Smith Blvd., Oranjestad ✛ Just before airport compound.

🍴 Restaurants

★ Barefoot

$$$ | CONTEMPORARY | Chef Gerco Aan het Rot and maître d' and sommelier Luc Beerepoot excel at pairing creative cuisine and upscale wine choices with the ultimate in a barefoot-luxury setting. Their menu of international fusion cuisine is also complemented by a choice of superb signature cocktails. **Known for:** romantic toes-in-the-sand dining; creative fusions like lobster cappuccino bisque and grouper topped with mango cream cheese; sand on the floor, even in the indoor dining area. $ *Average main: $30* ⊠ *L. G. Smith Blvd. 1, Oranjestad* ✛ *On Surfside Beach* ☎ *297/588–9824* ⊕ *www.barefootaruba.com.*

BAZ-RRR Galleria & Brasserie

$$ | CARIBBEAN | A new unique concept for downtown Oranjestad, this combination art gallery, brasserie, and creative arts community center showcases local artists while serving locally sourced food and drinks (as much as possible). The brasserie features a plant-based fusion menu, with the option to add meat or fish to your dish. **Known for:** healthy locally sourced food and authentic Aruban dishes; cool events like " We Need Wine Wednesdays" and "Foodie Lunch Happy Hour"; excellent specialty coffees and teas with pastries and snacks. $ *Average main: $15* ⊠ *Emma Straat 3, Oranjestad* ☎ *297/564–1102* ⊗ *Closed Sun., no dinner Sat.–Thurs.*

★ Bistro De Suikertuin

$$ | INTERNATIONAL | This charming bistro dining spot is the quintessential meeting place for locals and visitors alike seeking great signature cocktails, creative tapas, quality coffee, and healthy lunch options, as well as a full dinner menu with dishes that range from chicken cordon bleu to beef tenderloin with Dutch potatoes. Suikertuin means "sugar garden" in Dutch and this spot is so named for the yellow sugar birds that frequent the courtyard behind this historic colonial heritage house. **Known for:** elegant royal high tea and high wine services; authentic Aruban and Indonesian dishes like keshi yena and nasi goreng; lovely shaded courtyard with big tables for group socializing. $ *Average main: $20* ⊠ *Wilhelminastraat 64, Oranjestad* ☎ *297/582–6322* ⊗ *Closed Sun.*

★ Cuba's Cookin'

$$$ | CUBAN | This red-hot landmark establishment in the heart of Renaissance Marketplace specializes in traditional Havana specialties and is the only spot on Aruba where you can enjoy Cuban breakfast and an authentic Cuban sandwich for lunch. Their boast of having the best mojitos in town is a fair claim, and there's even

Most Aruba restaurants are casual and fun places for a drink and a meal.

a surprisingly good selection of gluten-free, vegetarian, and vegan fare on offer. **Known for:** melt-in-your-mouth ropa vieja (Cuba's national skirt steak dish); hot live music and alfresco dancing seven nights a week; an impressive selection of original Cuban art. $ *Average main: $28* ⊠ *Renaissance Marketplace, L. G. Smith Blvd. 82, Oranjestad* ☎ *297/588–0627* ⊕ *www.cubascookin.com.*

Driftwood

$$$ | CARIBBEAN | FAMILY | Opened in 1986, this rustic, nautical-themed restaurant is owned and operated by the Merryweather family. It's justifiably famous for serving up the freshest catch of the day caught by the owners themselves. **Known for:** family-recipe, hearty fish soup; boat-to-table fresh fish and other seafood; friendly service and warm atmosphere. $ *Average main: $30* ⊠ *Klipstraat 12, Oranjestad* ☎ *297/583–2515* ⊕ *www.driftwoodaruba.com* ☉ *Closed Sun.*

★ The Dutch Pancakehouse

$$ | DUTCH | FAMILY | Dutch pancakes are unlike North American-style flapjacks since they can be both savory and sweet, offering opportunities for breakfast, lunch, and dinner, and this legendary spot in the Renaissance Marketplace is considered the absolute best place to try them. More like thin crepes, they can be covered in (or stuffed with) a multitude of ingredients, which might include meats, vegetables, and cheeses. **Known for:** over 50 styles of sweet and savory Dutch-style pancakes; a surprising selection of excellent schnitzels; consistently good-quality fare and friendly service. $ *Average main: $15* ⊠ *Renaissance*

Marketplace, L. G. Smith Blvd. 9, Oranjestad ☎ *297/583–7180* ⊕ *www.thedutchpancakehouse.com.*

El Gaucho Argentine Grill

$$$$ | STEAKHOUSE | FAMILY | Aruba's original go-to mecca for carnivores since 1977, El Gaucho is famous for meat served in mammoth portions. Though to be honest, it's not all about meat; seafood platters are something to consider as well. **Known for:** 16-ounce Gaucho steak; largest shish kebab on the island; strolling musicians who create a fun and boisterous atmosphere. ⑤ *Average main: $40* ⊠ *Wilhelminastraat 80, Oranjestad* ☎ *297/582–3677* ⊕ *www.elgaucho-aruba.com* ☉ *Closed Sun.*

Fred

$$$$ | INTERNATIONAL | Chef Fred Wanders offers a chef's table experience in downtown Oranjestad with a five-course surprise menu in an intimate venue that seems more like his home kitchen than a dining spot. Optional wine pairings cost extra but are available by the glass and can be added to any course (or all courses). **Known for:** an intimate and excellent dining experience; creative international cuisine; reservations required, and adults-only. ⑤ *Average main:* ⊠ *Wilhelminastraat 18, Oranjestad* ✛ *Upstairs from Que Pasa restaurant* ☎ *297/565–2324* ⊕ *www.fredaruba. com* ☉ *Closed weekends.*

14 Bis Marketplace

$$ | INTERNATIONAL | This is a good choice for breakfast, lunch, or an early dinner (they close at 6 pm) if you need to be at the Queen Beatrix airport (they are located beside the airport entrance, but not inside so you don't actually have to be flying to eat here). The owners have hit on a winning concept: food sold by the kilo from a large, market-style buffet that includes both hot and cold dishes, as well as healthy to-go options that are more gently priced than the restaurants inside the terminal. **Known for:** healthy to-go options; an eclectic selection of vegan and vegetarian options; reasonable prices. ⑤ *Average main: $15* ⊠ *Queen Beatrix International Airport, Reina Beatrix Airport* ☎ *297/588–1440* ⊕ *14bisaruba. com.*

Gostoso Restaurante

$$$ | CARIBBEAN | FAMILY | Locals adore the magical mixture of Portuguese, Aruban, and international dishes on offer at this consistently excellent establishment. The decor walks a fine line between kitschy and cozy, but the atmosphere is relaxed and informal and outdoor seating is available. **Known for:** hearty Venezuelan-style mixed grill; large choice of authentic Aruba stobas (stews); popular local hangout. ⑤ *Average main: $28* ⊠ *Caya Ing. Roland H. Lacle 12, Oranjestad* ☎ *297/588–0053* ☉ *Closed Mon.*

L. G. Smith's Steak & Chop House

$$$$ | **STEAKHOUSE** | A study in teak, cream, and black, this fine steak house offers some of the best beef on the island. Subdued lighting and cascading water create an elegant atmosphere, and the view over the harbor makes for an exceptional dining experience. **Known for:** USDA-certified Angus beef; excellent wine list and stellar signature cocktails; Friday nights are Kobe nights. ⑤ *Average main: $50* ⊠ *Renaissance Aruba Marina Resort & Casino, L. G. Smith Blvd. 82, Oranjestad* ☎ *297/523–6195* ⊕ *www.lgsmiths.com.*

★ Pinchos Grill & Bar

$$$$ | **ECLECTIC** | One of the most romantic settings on the island is highlighted by enchanting twinkling lights strung over the water on a pier. *Pinchos* ("skewers" in Spanish) offers a fairly extensive menu of both meat and seafood skewers in addition to more creative main courses. Boursin-and-apple-stuffed pork tenderloin and fish cakes with pineapple-mayonnaise dressing and tomato salsa also keep customers coming back for more. **Known for:** romantic pier-side atmosphere; signature sangria; excellent personalized service. ⑤ *Average main: $35* ⊠ *L. G. Smith Blvd. 7, Oranjestad* ☎ *297/583–2666* ⊕ *www.pinchosaruba.com* ☺ *No lunch.*

Qué Pasa?

$$$ | **ECLECTIC** | This funky eatery is also part art gallery, and despite the name, the menu here is not Mexican but much more international with some real surprises like Peking duck, kangaroo tenderloin, and braised neck of lamb. The staff is helpful and friendly, and creative chef specials change daily. **Known for:** colorful decor and original Aruban artwork; an eclectic assortment of international dishes; fun and friendly atmosphere. ⑤ *Average main: $30* ⊠ *Wilhelminastraat 18, Oranjestad* ☎ *297/583–4888* ⊕ *www. quepasaaruba.com* ☺ *No lunch.*

Reflexions Beach Bar & Restaurant

MUSIC CLUBS | A sophisticated upscale spot on the water minutes from downtown Oranjestad does its best to replicate the South Beach Miami scene with luxe cabanas and daybeds, and beach and pool service around a chic seaside bar. It can be lively at nights when there are events, but dinner is mostly laid-back in high style with a good selection of quality cuts of meats and fresh fish and seafood, plus a good selection of fine champagnes. Daytime snacks and lunch offer up some interesting shareables and tapas, and there's a kids' menu. ⊠ *L. G. Smith Blvd. 1A, Surfside Beach, Oranjestad* ☎ *297/582–0153* ⊕ *www.reflexionsaruba.com.*

Restaurant Anno 1887

$$ | FRENCH | Those still mourning the loss of two of Aruba's most beloved dining spots—Chez Mathilde and Le Dome—can dry their eyes, because some of the original players of those establishments have teamed up to create the same type of classic French experience in downtown Oranjestad. Expect impeccable personal service and iconic French fare like *tournedos au poivre* (beef in red wine) and coq au vin. **Known for:** Classic French dishes like bouillabaisse de Marseille and chocolate or Grand Marnier soufflé; quality ingredients always prepared "a la minute"; prix-fixe five-course chef tasting menu. ⑤ *Average main: $25* ✉ *Wilheminastraat 27, Oranjestad* ☎ *297/583–0020* ⊕ *www.restaurantanno1877.com* ✆ *Closed Mon. and Tues.*

Surfside Beach Bar

$ | INTERNATIONAL | FAMILY | Enjoy cool and creative cocktails and beach shack eats in the afternoon on a pristine stretch of white sand on an aqua sea just minutes from downtown Oranjestad. The fun and friendly vibe includes beach service, lounge and umbrella rentals, and happy hour drink specials. **Known for:** Sunday barbecue noon–7 pm; casual fare like burgers, spicy shrimp, fish-and-chips, and create-your-own pizzas; hearty Dutch-style breakfasts Friday–Sunday. ⑤ *Average main: $12* ✉ *Surfside Beach, Oranjestad* ☎ *297/280–6584* ⊕ *www.surfsidearuba.com.*

★ Taste My Aruba

$$$$ | CARIBBEAN | What began as a teeny-tiny café dedicated to serving up creative twists on authentic local fare and specialty coffee and treats for lunch in 2018 has become an unlikely hot spot for fresh fish and local lobster dinners thanks to the personality and culinary skills of its owner-chef Nathalie de Mey. The unique preparations of the catch of the day fill up the sidewalk tables, so be sure to make dinner reservations. **Known for:** expertly prepared giant local lobster and fresh fish straight from the boat; authentic local experience and locally sourced fare; surprising selection of unique Argentinean wines. ⑤ *Average main: $32* ✉ *Cosecha Building, Zoutman Straat 1, Oranjestad* ⚐ *Tucked beneath the Cosecha building* ☎ *297/749–1600* ⊕ *www.tastemyaruba.com* ✆ *Closed Sun.*

The West Deck

$$ | CARIBBEAN | FAMILY | Opened by the same people who own Pinchos, this fun, friendly, wood-decked grill joint offers casual fare like barbecue ribs and grilled shrimp by the dozen, as well as Caribbean bites like jerk wings, fried *funchi* (like a thick polenta) with Dutch cheese, and West Indian samosas. There are some surprisingly snazzy dishes, too, like lobster-crab cocktail with red grapefruit and cognac cream drizzle. **Known for:** a great pit stop along the Linear Park; Beer-Ritas; superb sunset views on Surfside Beach. $ *Average main: $20* ⊠ *L. G. Smith Blvd., at Governor's Bay, Oranjestad* ☎ *297/587–2667* ⊕ *www.thewestdeck.com.*

Wilhelmina

$$$$ | **INTERNATIONAL** | Choose from a simple and elegant indoor dining area or a tropical outdoor garden oasis to sample from the creative international menu that includes choices of quality meats, homemade pastas, and fresh fish and seafood, all with suggested wine pairings from the well-regarded cellar. The menu also includes an impressive offering of avant-garde vegetarian dishes. **Known for:** creative takes on conventional dishes like a signature salad with rock lobster and scallops; excellent selection of fine wines; exotic mains like Surinamese sea bass and Indonesian-style roast pork. $ *Average main: $40* ⊠ *Wilhelmenastraat 74, Oranjestad* ☎ *297/583–7445* ⊕ *www.wilhelminaaruba.com* ☾ *Closed Mon.*

Hotels

★ Renaissance Aruba Ocean Suites

$$$ | **RESORT** | **FAMILY** | Spacious suites attract families and groups to this downtown resort that offers its own man-made beach on the sea and free water taxi to its lovely private island minutes away. **Pros:** private island access; spacious water circuit and stellar sea views; steps from downtown. **Cons:** limited dining on-site; limited water sports; can be noisy at night as it's right downtown. $ *Rooms from: $450* ⊠ *Renaissance Beach, L. G. Smith Blvd., Oranjestad* ☎ *297/583–6000* ⊕ *www.renaissancearubaresortand-casino.com* ⇆ *259 rooms* ◉ *Free Breakfast.*

Renaissance Aruba Resort and Casino: Marina Hotel

$$$ | **HOTEL** | Completely renovated in 2017, the adults-only side of the Aruba Renaissance twin resorts offers guests a chic, waterfront urban oasis in the heart of downtown Oranjestad, including water taxi access to a luxurious private island beach. **Pros:** in the heart of the best downtown shopping and dining; good choice of in-hotel nightlife and restaurants and in-house casino; beautiful private island beach with deluxe cabana rentals. **Cons:** rooms are small and have no balconies; marina pool is tiny; nights can be noisy. $ *Rooms from: $450* ⊠ *L. G. Smith Blvd. 82, Oranjestad* ☎ *297/583–6000, 800/421–8188* ⊕ *www.renaissancearuba.com* ⇆ *297 rooms* ◉ *Free Breakfast.*

⊙ Nightlife

Businesses come and go in the alfresco Renaissance Marketplace on the marina, but it's always a lively hot spot after the dinner hour, when most of the cafés, bistros, and restaurants transform the vibe with their own live music or entertainment. The sparkling lights on the water and the live bands playing in the common square every evening also add to the magic. Spots like Cuba's Cookin, Café the Plaza, and others often have special events. This is also the spot where pop-up festivals will be found at night. It's a popular gathering spot for locals as well as visitors.

It's not a bar, but landmark snack spot Djiespie's Place is worth a mention because there's a street party in the courtyard every Friday night at 6 pm. It's an authentic Aruba night out and visitors are welcome to join in.

BARS

★ Alfie's in Aruba

BARS/PUBS | Two Canadians bought this newly popular watering hole but they haven't forgotten their homeland; Canadian Moosehead beer and authentic Quebec-style poutine are just as readily available here as a Heineken or Corona. Also on tap are mega-burgers, Thursday rib nights, and live music every Friday. And, of course, you can watch hockey. Look for the giant Canadian flag outside. It's closed Monday. ⊠ *Dominicanessenstraat 10, Oranjestad* ☎ *297/569–5815* ⊕ *www.alfiesinaruba.com.*

★ BLUE

MUSIC CLUBS | Located steps away from the cool infinity pool of the Renaissance Marina Hotel, BLUE is one of the hippest social gathering spots on the island. It's the place where young local professionals gather for happy hour during the week. Later it morphs into a hot, nightly DJ-driven scene bathed in blue and violet lights with a giant video wall and talented barkeeps serving upscale concoctions like their signature Blue Solo Martini. ⊠ *Renaissance Marina Hotel, L. G. Smith Blvd. 82, Oranjestad* ☎ *297/ 583–6000* ⊕ *www.renaissancearubaresortandcasino.com.*

Cafe Chaos

MUSIC CLUBS | This is not so much a "dance club" as a place to dance and let loose for mostly local Dutch expats. The no-nonsense bar offers a wide variety of music, from live bands to DJs spanning styles from reggae to funk to rock. It's a mix, and it all depends on the mood of the crowd and the night. But it's a great spot to make new local friends. The live music often starts very late, but you can happen upon some crazy jam sessions, too. ⊠ *L. G. Smith Blvd. 60, Oranjestad* ☎ *297/588–7547* ⊕ *www.cafechaosaruba.com.*

★ Eetcafe The Paddock

BARS/PUBS | It's impossible to miss the big red roof just off the marina, especially since there is a large Holstein cow and an entire car sitting on top of it! But that's the point. Wild, crazy, and whimsical is their claim to fame, and there's no better spot in town to catch Dutch "futball" if you're seeking the craziest orange-clad die-hard fans. Though it's a popular tourist lunch spot during the day, this joint really morphs into party-hearty mode at night, full of carousing locals and visitors alike enjoying the great deals on drinks via the late-night happy hours and dollar-beer specials. Live music often adds to the revelry. ⊠ *L. G. Smith Blvd. 13, Oranjestad* ☎ *297/583–2334* ⊕ *www.paddockaruba.com.*

Garufa Cocktail Lounge

BARS/PUBS | After closing a few years back, and hosting a few temporary pop-up bars, this legendary little cigar lounge reopened in 2019. Look for the mustard and white colonial building with the Juliette balcony to find a friendly gang of locals and visitors enjoying top-shelf spirits, creative signature cocktails, tapas, and quality cigars. A powerful smoke-extractor system helps keep the air clear and late night happy hour runs from 9 to 11 pm. ⊠ *Wilhelminastraat 63, Oranjestad* ☎ *297/582–7205.*

Iguana Joe's Caribbean Bar & Grill

BARS/PUBS | The colorful and creative reptilian-themed decor makes this a favorite hangout for cruise visitors who want to enjoy the view of the port from the second-floor balcony while enjoying sangria and massive frozen cocktails. Dinner is served, and the food deserves recognition (especially the jerk chicken and coconut shrimp), but the bar is the real draw as people come to people-watch and sample the potent drink list, especially their signature Pink Iguana. ⊠ *Royal Plaza Mall, L. G. Smith Blvd. 94, Oranjestad* ☎ *297/583–9373* ⊕ *www.iguanajoesaruba.com* ✆ *Closed Sun.*

Lucy's Retired Surfers Bar & Restaurant

BARS/PUBS | It may not be on the beach, but Lucy's has the quintessential beach bar vibe and there is a small man-made beach area outside replete with hammocks. By day it's a lunch spot serving up burgers and hearty American fare, but it ramps up the vibe at happy hour and then becomes a hot nightlife spot later with live music and creative drink specials. They are also one of Aruba's only officially dog-friendly bars! ⊠ *Renaissance Marina, L. G. Smith Blvd. 82, Oranjestad* ☎ *297/280–1970* ⊕ *www.lucyssurf. com.*

7 West HotShotz

DANCE CLUBS | Named after its address this is predominantly an eatery for lunch and casual dinner in the early evening until the lights dim later on to reveal a seriously cool neon glow-in-the-dark interior that attracts a local crowd of thirsty folks seeking signature cocktails amid hot music in downtown Oranjestad. Shooter specials, theme nights, hot DJs, and cool cocktails keep the party going, as do late-night happy hours. ⊠ *Weststraat 7, Oranjestad* ☎ *297/588–9983.*

★ The West Deck Island Grill Beach Bar

BARS/PUBS | Just over the wooden walkway from Renaissance Ocean Suites along the Linear Park you'll find this casual wooden deck beach bar on the water that's called Governor's Bay. Enjoy one of their special upside-down margaritas or incredible craft cocktails while you catch a stellar sunset and watch the cruise ships go by. After dark, the music takes it up a notch—sometimes live—and the atmosphere is fun and friendly. It's as popular with locals as it is with visitors. Great Caribbean tapas and grilled specialties are also on tap. ⊠ *Governor's Bay Oranjestad, L. G. Smith Blvd.* ✛ *Linear Park (next to the Queen Wilhelmina Park, adjacent to the Renaissance Suites)* ☎ *297/587–2667* ⊕ *www. thewestdeck.com.*

WEEKLY PARTIES

★ Bon Bini Festival

FESTIVALS | This year-round folklore event (the name means "welcome" in Papiamento) is held every Tuesday from 6:30 pm to 8:30 pm at Ft. Zoutman in Oranjestad. In the inner courtyard, you can check out the Antillean dancers in resplendent costumes, feel the rhythms of the steel drums, browse among the stands displaying local artwork, and sample local food and drink. ⊠ *Fort Zoutman, Oranjestad* ⊕ *www.aruba.com* ✄ *$5.*

🎭 Performing Arts

Aruba has a handful of not-so-famous but very talented performers. Over the years, several local artists, including composer Julio Renado Euson, choreographer Wilma Kuiperi, sculptor Ciro Abath, and visual artist Elvis Lopez, have gained international renown. Furthermore, many Aruban musicians play more than one type of music (classical, jazz, soca, salsa, reggae, calypso, rap, pop), and many compose as well as perform. Edjean Semeleer has followed in the footsteps of his mentor Padu Lampe—the composer of the island's national anthem and a beloved local star—to become one of the island's best-loved entertainers. His performances pack Aruba's biggest halls, especially his annual Christmas concert. He

This popular photo-op spot can be found in downtown Oranjestad.

sings in many languages, and though he's young, his style is old-style crooner—Aruba's answer to Michael Bublé.

Cas Di Cultura
ARTS CENTERS | The National Theater of Aruba, the island's cultural center, hosts art exhibits, folkloric shows, dance performances, and concerts throughout the year. ✉ *Vondellaan 2, Oranjestad* ☎ *297/582–1010* ⊕ *www.casdicultura.aw.*

UNOCA
ARTS CENTERS | Although UNOCA is Aruba's national gallery, it's much more, acting as an anchor to host cultural and performance events, which are often held here. ✉ *Stadionweg 21, Oranjestad* ☎ *297/583–5681* ⊕ *www.unocaruba.org.*

ANNUAL ARTS FESTIVALS
Finally, the island's many festivals showcase arts and culture. To find out what's going on, check out the local English-language newspapers or look for events online at ⊕ *aruba.com.*

Shopping

Oranjestad's original "Main Street" (behind the Renaissance Marina Resort) has seen a massive renovation of the entire downtown region, which has breathed new life into the backstreets, adding pedestrian-only stretches, compact malls, and open resting areas. A free eco-trolley now loops throughout downtown, allowing you to hop on and off to shop and stroll. Stores selling fashions, souvenirs, specialty items, sporting goods, and cosmetics can all be found on this renewed street, along with plenty of cafés, snack spots, and outdoor terraces, where you can catch your breath between retail therapy jaunts.

CIGARS
Cigar Emporium
TOBACCO | The Cubans come straight from the climate-controlled humidor at Cigar Emporium. Choose from Cohiba, Montecristo, Romeo y Julieta, Partagas, and more. ⊠ *Renaissance Mall, L. G. Smith Blvd. 82, Oranjestad* ☎ *297/582–5479.*

CLOTHING AND ACCESSORIES
★ Gucci
SHOES/LUGGAGE/LEATHER GOODS | What's in a name? When the name is Gucci, you know it's always trendsetting top quality. The sophisticated store offers fashions for men and women as well as their distinctive luxury shoes, handbags, leather goods, eyewear, and accessories. ⊠ *Renaissance Mall, L. G. Smith Blvd. 82, Oranjestad* ☎ *297/583–3952* ⊕ *www.gucci.com.*

★ Mango
CLOTHING | A complete makeover to match the downtown restoration has turned this popular Spanish chain outlet into a megastore that now dominates the block along the trolley tracks on Main Street. It offers multiple levels of air-conditioned, fashion-forward shopping for all ages. Plus-size fashions are available, too. It's as popular with the locals as it is with visitors. ⊠ *Caya Betico Croes 9, Oranjestad* ☎ *297/582–9800* ⊕ *shop.mango.com.*

Tommy Hilfiger
CLOTHING | The activewear sold at Tommy Hilfiger makes this a great stop for a vacation wardrobe. A Tommy Jeans store is also there. There are also stores in the Renaissance Mall and Paseo Herencia Mall on the high-rise resort strip. ⊠ *Royal Plaza Mall, L. G. Smith Blvd. 94, Oranjestad* ☎ *297/583–8548* ⊕ *global.tommy.com.*

DUTY-FREE STORES
Dufry
JEWELRY/ACCESSORIES | No doubt you've seen this brand of duty-free stores in airports all over the world, but don't expect to see the same duty-free items like tobacco and spirits in this one, and the prices are not completely duty-free. What you will find are great bargains on cosmetics, perfumes, jewelry, and accessories from such brands as Carolina Herrara, Calvin Klein, Armani, Montblanc, and more. And there's always some kind of major sale on something of good quality going on there. There's another

outlet in Royal Plaza Mall. ⊠ *G. F. Betico Croes 29, Oranjestad* ☎ *297/582–2790* ⊕ *www.dufry.com.*

ELECTRONICS
★ Boolchand's Digital World

CAMERAS/ELECTRONICS | Family-run Boolchand's began in the 1930s and has since become a major retail institution throughout the Caribbean; they opened their first shop on Aruba in 1974. Today, their downtown "Digital World" is your one-stop shop to get a high-tech fix at seriously low prices. Top-quality merchandise by major brands includes the latest in computers, cameras, and tech accessories, as well as quality watches and Pandora jewelry. ⊠ *Havenstraat 25, Oranjestad* ☎ *297/583–0147* ⊕ *www.boolchand.com.*

FOOD
Ling & Sons IGA Super Center

FOOD/CANDY | Always a family-owned and family-operated grocery company, Ling and Sons adopted the IGA-brand supermarket style with all the goods you would expect in an IGA back home. In addition to a wide variety of foods, there's a bakery, a deli, a butcher shop, and a well-stocked "liquortique." You can also order your groceries online to be delivered to your hotel room. Ask about their VIP card for discounts. ⊠ *Schotlandstraat 41, Oranjestad* ☎ *297/521–2370* ⊕ *www.lingandsons.com.*

GIFTS AND SOUVENIRS
★ The Mask—Mopa Mopa Art

GIFTS/SOUVENIRS | These shops specialize in original masks and crafty items called mopa mopa art. Originating with the Quillacingas people of Ecuador and Colombia, the art is made from the bud of the mopa mopa tree, boiled down into a resin, colored with dyes, and applied to carved mahogany and other woods like cedar. Masks, jewelry boxes, coasters, whimsical animal figurines, and more make wonderfully unique gifts and souvenirs. The masks are also believed to ward off evil spirits. Find them in Paseo Herencia Mall, Royal Plaza Mall, and Renaissance Marketplace. You can also buy works online. ⊠ *Renaissance Marketplace, L. G. Smith Blvd. 9, Oranjestad* ☎ *297/588–7297* ⊕ *www.mopamopaaruba.com.*

JEWELRY
★ Colombian Emeralds International

JEWELRY/ACCESSORIES | A trusted international jewelry dealer specializing in emeralds, this outlet also has a top-notch selection of diamonds, sapphire, tanzanite, rubies, ammolite, pearls, gold, semiprecious gems, luxury watches, and more at very competitive prices. A highly professional and knowledgeable staff adds to their credibility. (They also have a duty-free store in the airport.)

✉ *Renaissance Mall, L. G. Smith Blvd. 82, Oranjestad* ☎ *297/583–6238* ⊕ *www.colombianemeralds.com.*

★ Diamonds International

JEWELRY/ACCESSORIES | One of the pioneer diamond retailers in the Caribbean with over 125 stores throughout the chain, the Aruba outlet has been operating in the same spot since 1997, and you can't miss the mammoth store as soon as you step off a cruise ship. The company is well-known for their expertise, selection, quality, and competitive prices on diamonds, and they also sell high-end timepieces. The founders of Diamonds International are both graduates of the Gemological Institute of America. You'll find smaller outlets in many of the island's top resorts. ✉ *L. G. Smith Blvd. 17, Oranjestad* ☎ *800/515–3935* ⊕ *www.diamondsinternational.com.*

Gandelman Jewelers

JEWELRY/ACCESSORIES | Established in 1936, this family-run store is one of the island's premier jewelers. It's also Aruba's official Rolex retailer and the exclusive agent for names like Cartier (the only official retailer on the island), Patek Philippe, and David Yurman. There are two other stores on Aruba in the Aruba Marriott and the Aruba Hyatt Regency in addition to this flagship. ✉ *Renaissance Mall, L. G. Smith Blvd. 82, Oranjestad* ☎ *297/529–9000* ⊕ *www.gandelman.net.*

★ Kay's Fine Jewelry

JEWELRY/ACCESSORIES | Kay's family-run emporium is a well-known Aruba fixture on the fine-jewelry scene, and their designs have won awards. Exquisite settings featuring white and colored diamonds are their claim to fame, and they also have a fine selection of precious gems and brand-name timepieces. ✉ *Westraat 8, Oranjestad* ☎ *297/588–9978* ⊕ *www.kaysfinejewelry.com.*

Little Switzerland

PERFUME/COSMETICS | With four stores on the island—mostly in high-rise resorts and the original location in downtown Royal Plaza Mall—these well-known outlets specialize in designer jewelry and upscale timepieces by big-name designers like TAG Heuer, David Yurman, Breitling, Roberto Coin, Chopard, Pandora, Tiffany & Co., Cartier, Movado, Omega, and John Hardy. They also own the TAG Heuer Boutique in Renaissance Mall. ✉ *Royal Plaza Mall, L. G. Smith Blvd. 94, Oranjestad* ☎ *844/332–4415* ⊕ *www.littleswitzerland.com.*

Did You Know?

Established in 1933, the Aruba Trading Company is located in the gorgeous Dutch colonial structure known as La Casa Amarilla (The Yellow House) in downtown Oranjestad.

MALLS AND MARKETPLACES
★ Renaissance Mall
CLOTHING | Upscale, name-brand fashion and luxury brands of perfume, cosmetics, and leather goods are what you'll find in the array of 60 stores spanning two floors in this mall located within and underneath the Renaissance Marina Resort. You'll also find specialty items like cigars and designer shoes plus high-end gold, silver, diamonds, and quality jewelry at low- or no-duty prices. Cafés and high-end dining, plus a casino and spa, round out the offerings. Shopping until 8 pm daily. ⊠ *Renaissance Marina Resort, L. G. Smith Blvd. 82, Oranjestad* ☎ *297/582–4622* ⊕ *www.shoprenaissancearuba.com.*

★ Renaissance Marketplace
SHOPPING CENTERS/MALLS | FAMILY | The Renaissance Marketplace is more of a dining and gathering spot along the marina than a market. It's a lively spot with a few souvenir shops and specialty stores. There is also a modern cinema. But mostly it's full of eclectic dining emporiums and trendy cafés, and they have live music some weekends in their alfresco square. The Wind Creek Seaport casino is also there, and it's steps from the cruise terminal on the marina. It also is the place for the big annual Christmas Fair. ⊠ *L. G. Smith Blvd. 82, Oranjestad* ☎ *297/582–4622* ⊕ *www.renaissancearubaresortandcasino.com.*

Royal Plaza Mall
SHOPPING CENTERS/MALLS | It's impossible to miss this gorgeous colonial-style, cotton-candy-colored building with the big gold dome gracing the front street along the marina. It's one of the most photographed in Oranjestad. Three levels of shops (both indoors and out) make up this artsy arcade full of small boutiques, cigar shops, designer clothing outlets, gift and jewelry stores, and souvenir kiosks. Great dining and bars are found within as well. ⊠ *L. G. Smith Blvd. 94, Oranjestad* ☎ *297/588–0351* ⊕ *www. aruba.com.*

PERFUMES AND COSMETICS
Penha, Dufry, Little Switzerland, and Maggy's are all known for their extensive fragrance offerings.

Penha
CLOTHING | Originating in Curaçao in 1865, Penha has branched out throughout the Caribbean and has eight stores on Aruba. The largest is right next to the Renaissance Marina Hotel. The store is particularly known for good prices on high-end perfumes, cosmetics, skin-care products, eyewear, and fashions. You'll find brand names such as MAC, Lancôme, Estée Lauder, Clinique, Chanel,

Dior, Montblanc, and Victoria's Secret to name just a few. There's another location in Palm Beach Plaza. ⊠ *Caya G. F. Betico Croes 11/13, Oranjestad* ☎ *297/582–0082* ⊕ *www.jlpenha.com.*

SPAS
★ Okeanos Spa

SPA/BEAUTY | The full-service spa at the Renaissance Marina Hotel is well equipped to help you relax to the max, but the incredible seaside palapa cove on private Renaissance Island is the best venue for a relaxing massage or treatment. It's accessible by free water taxi when you book a treatment, and your purchase also gains you access to the stellar protected coves and white-sand beaches. Access to the island is otherwise limited to Renaissance guests. There is a beach bar and a full-service restaurant on-site, so you can make an entire blissful day of it. ⊠ *Renaissance Aruba Resort & Casino, L. G. Smith Blvd. 82, Oranjestad* ☎ *297/583–6000* ⊕ *www.renaissancearubaspa.com.*

MANCHEBO, DRUIF, AND EAGLE BEACHES

Updated by
Sue Campbell

⊙ Sights   🍴 Restaurants   🛏 Hotels   ⊖ Shopping   🍸 Nightlife
★★★☆☆   ★★★★☆   ★★★★★   ★★☆☆☆   ★★☆☆☆

NEIGHBORHOOD SNAPSHOT

TOP EXPERIENCES

- **Stroll Silky Sand:** Take long romantic walks along a carpet of silky white sand capped with fiery sunsets.

- **Dine Out in Style:** Choose from an eclectic array of unique dining locations: barefoot on the beach, in a canopied bed, or at an intimate chef's table.

- **Pamper Body and Soul:** Join beachfront yoga classes under giant shade palapas and enjoy a luxurious seaside massage to ease the muscles.

- **Dance Under the Stars:** Head to Alhambra Mall and Casino for live music at the alfresco restaurants and bars.

- **Golf with Nature:** Play a picturesque round of golf amid ocean-view greens and beautifully landscaped lagoons full of wildlife.

- **De-Stress:** Relax and read a book while swaying in a seaside hammock or do nothing but swim and sunbathe in quiet bliss.

GETTING HERE AND AROUND

The Eagle Beach region—also known as the low-rise section—is actually three beaches connected to each other, beginning right between the tip of downtown Oranjestad just past the cruise-ship terminal and ending at the Bubali wetlands just before the Divi Aruba Phoenix. It's about a 15- to 20-minute drive from the airport (depending on traffic through Oranjestad) and it's accessible by public bus from the downtown terminal. Buses run regularly and stop at every major resort area along the coast. There is plenty of free parking along the beaches.

QUICK BITES

- **Santos Coffee with Soul.** Behind the Alhambra Mall, this is an ideal spot to get your gourmet coffee fix and grab some bagels and sandwiches to go before a beach day. ⊠ *J. E. Irausquin Blvd. 51, Eagle Beach* ⊕ *www.santos-aruba.com*

- **Beach Bar.** Located across the street from Divi Village Golf & Beach Resort, this beachside spot serves the perfect beach fare—panini, wraps, and salads—as well as great cocktails and live entertainment. ⊠ *Druif Beach* ⊕ *www.diviresorts.com*

- **Pizza Bob's Restaurant & Pub.** Grab a Chicago-style slice or a cocktail at this friendly alfresco hideaway beside the Alhambra Mall. ⊠ *J. E. Irausquin Blvd. 57, Eagle Beach* ⊕ *pizzabobsaua.weebly.com*

Unlike the action-packed party that is Palm Beach, Eagle Beach is where you go to unwind, relax, recharge, and rejuvenate in pristine postcard-perfect settings. Once you experience it, you'll see why it's consistently rated among the top three beaches on the planet, and you'll want to go back.

Nearby, an entire village of Divi Resorts encompasses Druif Beach, while Manchebo Beach is the broadest stretch of sand on the island. It's become the spot for health and wellness retreats, and it's known to have the most eco-friendly hotel in the entire Caribbean.

⊙ Sights

There are few attractions or historic sites in this area. Pastimes are purely sun and sand oriented with sunset strolls and toes-in-the-sand dining entertainment, enough for those who choose to stay in the low-rise region; activities typically center around the respective resorts.

The area's most famous site is the iconic fofoti tree on Eagle Beach. It's the island's most photographed tree, and the one that you so often see in Aruba's marketing and promotions.
■TIP→ **This tree is often mistakenly referred to as a divi-divi tree; though similar, they are not the same species.**

CASINOS
★ Alhambra Casino
CASINO—SIGHT | Part of the Divi family and accessible by golf cart from the company's all-inclusive resorts, this is a lively popular casino with a big selection of modern slots, blackjack, craps, poker, roulette, and more. Be sure to join their Player's Club—it's free and offers free slot credits, and you earn points with your card as well. The Cove restaurant serves light meals and drinks; you'll also receive free drinks on the floor when you're playing the games. Special theme nights and promotions run all week, and on Saturday afternoon the casino hosts Super Bingo. ⊠ *L. G. Smith Blvd. 47, Druif* ☎ *297/583–5000* ⊕ *www.casinoalhambra.com.*

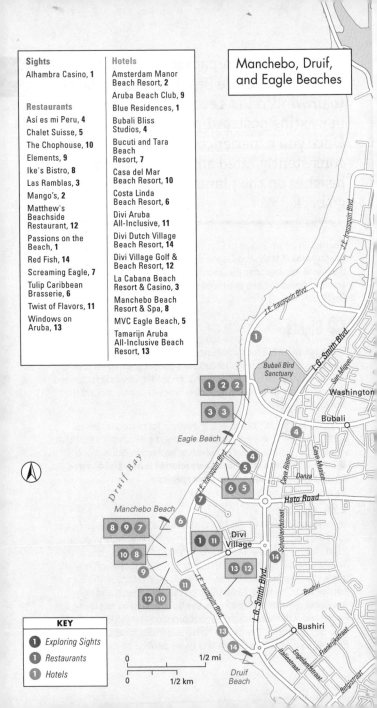

Sights
Alhambra Casino, **1**

Restaurants
Así es mi Peru, **4**
Chalet Suisse, **5**
The Chophouse, **10**
Elements, **9**
Ike's Bistro, **8**
Las Ramblas, **3**
Mango's, **2**
Matthew's Beachside Restaurant, **12**
Passions on the Beach, **1**
Red Fish, **14**
Screaming Eagle, **7**
Tulip Caribbean Brasserie, **6**
Twist of Flavors, **11**
Windows on Aruba, **13**

Hotels
Amsterdam Manor Beach Resort, **2**
Aruba Beach Club, **9**
Blue Residences, **1**
Bubali Bliss Studios, **4**
Bucuti and Tara Beach Resort, **7**
Casa del Mar Beach Resort, **10**
Costa Linda Beach Resort, **6**
Divi Aruba All-Inclusive, **11**
Divi Dutch Village Beach Resort, **14**
Divi Village Golf & Beach Resort, **12**
La Cabana Beach Resort & Casino, **3**
Manchebo Beach Resort & Spa, **8**
MVC Eagle Beach, **5**
Tamarijn Aruba All-Inclusive Beach Resort, **13**

Manchebo, Druif, and Eagle Beaches

J.E. Irausquin Blvd
L.G. Smith Blvd
San Miguel
Washington
Bubali
Bubali Bird Sanctuary
Cava Ronde
Cava Musica
Eagle Beach
Danza
Hato Road
Druif Bay
Sero landstraat
Manchebo Beach
Divi Village
Bushiri
Bushiri
Druif Beach
Engelandstraat
Italiestraat
Frankrijkstraat
Belgiestraat

KEY
1 Exploring Sights
1 Restaurants
1 Hotels

0 — 1/2 mi
0 — 1/2 km

Beaches

Aruba's low-rise region is lined with beautiful beaches. Some have adopted the names of the resorts they are famous for: Manchebo Beach is technically the beginning of Eagle Beach, and Divi Beach is still Druif Beach, named for the type of trees that used to grow in abundance there. They join at Punta Brabo, which means rough point, and it's aptly named as the current and rip tides there can be severe and there's a quick drop-off. Eagle Beach continues in a long straight line afterward, and has often been named one of the world's top three beaches for good reason. Surf is usually gentle, but it can be occasionally rough too, so heed the warning flags as there are no lifeguards.

Druif Beach

BEACH—SIGHT | Fine white sand and calm water make this beach a great choice for sunbathing and swimming. It's the base beach for the Divi collections of all-inclusive resorts, so amenities are reserved for guests. But the locals like it, too, and often camp out here as well with their own chairs and coolers. The beach is accessible by bus, rental car, or taxi, and it's within easy walking distance to many stores for food and drinks. You can also buy coupons at the front desk of both resorts if you want to purchase food and drink from their facilities. **Amenities:** food and drink; toilets; parking (free); water sports. **Best for:** swimming; partiers. ⊠ *J. E. Irausquin Blvd., Druif* ⊹ *Near the Divi resorts, south of Punta Brabo.*

★ Eagle Beach

BEACH—SIGHT | Aruba's most photographed stretch of sand, Eagle Beach is not only a favorite with visitors and locals, but also of sea turtles. More sea turtles nest here than anywhere else on the island. This pristine stretch of blinding white sand and aqua surf is ranked among the best beaches in the world. Many of the hotels have facilities on or near the beach, and refreshments are never far away, but chairs and shade palapas are reserved for resort guests only. **Amenities:** food and drink; toilets; parking (no fee). **Best for:** sunsets; swimming; water sports. ⊠ *J. E. Irausquin Blvd., north of Manchebo Beach, Druif.*

★ Manchebo Beach (*Punta Brabo*)

BEACH—SIGHT | Impressively wide, the white-sand shoreline in front of the Manchebo Beach Resort (technically where Eagle Beach begins) is the backdrop for the numerous yoga classes now taking place under the giant palapa since the resort began offering health and wellness retreats. This sandy stretch is the broadest on the island; in fact you can even get a workout just getting to

Did You Know?

Hurricanes don't always cause beach erosion. When Hurricane Ivan passed north of Aruba in 2004 (one of the rare hurricanes that directly affected the island), Eagle Beach actually got a few feet wider.

the water! Waves can be rough and wild at certain times of the year, though, so mind the current and undertow when swimming. ■ TIP→ **The Bucuti beach bar no longer serves walk-ins and is now reserved exclusively for guests. Amenities:** food and drink; toilets. **Best for:** swimming; sunsets; walking. ⊠ *J. E. Irausquin Blvd., Druif* ⊹ *At Manchebo Beach Resort.*

⑪ Restaurants

The Eagle Beach region has an eclectic selection of dining options from high-end eateries to romantic private dining options and friendly beach bar haunts for burgers and barbecue. Many of the finest spots are part of a resort and are open to the public, but there are a few excellent stand-alone exceptions.

Asi es mi Peru

$$$ | PERUVIAN | Owner Roxanna Salinas has created an authentic Peruvian-style dining spot to share a taste of her home with locals and visitors alike. Authentic specialties are artfully served in a warm and colorful enclave, and a portion of proceeds from the wares sold at the on-site Peruvian craft market go to a local Aruban cancer foundation as well. **Known for:** Peruvian-style ceviche made table-side; vegetarian and vegan menu available; five-course chef's table sampling menu on request. ⑤ *Average main: $26* ⊠ *Paradise Beach Villas, J. E. Irausquin Blvd. 64, Eagle Beach* ☎ *297/592–5699* ⊕ *www.asiesmiperuenaruba.com* ☉ *Closed Mon.*

Chalet Suisse

$$$$ | EUROPEAN | Opened in 1988 as a re-created Swiss-style chalet, this is a perennial favorite for the time-share folks and repeat visitors due to its high-quality classic European dishes—chicken cordon bleu, beef Stroganoff, and duck à l'orange—as well as island-inspired favorites like stuffed, locally caught grouper medallions. They also have rotating seasonally inspired menus, and their low season early-bird menu is very popular. **Known for:** expertly prepared whole rack of lamb; rich Swiss chocolate fondue for dessert; excellent wine cellar. ⑤ *Average main: $40* ⊠ *J. E. Irausquin Blvd. 246, Eagle Beach* ☎ *297/587–5054* ⊕ *www.chaletsuisse-aruba.com* ☉ *Closed Sun.*

★ The Chophouse

$$$$ | INTERNATIONAL | Low-key elegance and soft piano music set the stage for this indoor enclave where meaty chops and steaks are king and classic silver service is still in vogue. The big surprise here though is the chic Omakase Japanese Sushi Bar that shares the space, and their selection of vegetarian, vegan,

and gluten-free options is impressive. **Known for:** premium steaks and chops; predominately organic and sustainable fare; elegant old-world atmosphere combined with a modern sushi bar. $ *Average main: $40 ⊠ Manchebo Resort, J. E. Irausquin Blvd. 55, Druif* ☎ *297/582–3444* ⊕ *www.thechophousearuba.com* ⊙ *Sushi bar closed Sun. and Mon.*

★ Elements

$$$$ | CONTEMPORARY | A stellar spot with stunning seaside views, Elements embodies the resort's reputation for promoting green living and a healthy lifestyle. The wide-ranging menu of internationally flavored dishes includes many organic, vegan, vegetarian, and gluten-free choices, and ingredients are locally sourced whenever possible. **Known for:** special Monday Aruban nights with a prix-fixe local specialty menu; romantic surf-side atmosphere with private prix-fixe palapa dining for two; excellent vegan options. $ *Average main: $40 ⊠ Bucuti and Tara Beach Resort, L. G. Smith Blvd. 55B, Eagle Beach* ☎ *297/583–1100* ⊕ *www.elementsaruba. com.*

★ Ike's Bistro

$$$ | INTERNATIONAL | Completely reimagined in 2018 as a contemporary poolside dining option at Manchebo Resort, the new menus and special nights are attracting people seeking inspired Caribbean-international cuisine, and vegans are especially excited about an entire menu devoted to gourmet plant-based dining. Creative preparations of meat, seafood, and fish—locally sourced whenever possible—are all enhanced with flavors from the on-site fresh herb garden, and the chef often surprises with exotic daily specials. **Known for:** paella night Thursday with Spanish music and live cooking; lobster night Monday; four-course chef's surprise tasting menu, with or without wine. $ *Average main: $30 ⊠ Manchebo Beach Resort, J. E. Irausquin Blvd. 55, Druif* ☎ *297/522–3444* ⊕ *www.ikesbistro.com.*

Las Ramblas

$$$ | SPANISH | This small alfresco Spanish-theme restaurant at La Cabana is often off-radar for anyone that's not a guest at the resort, but it's worth seeking out for excellent charcoal-grilled steaks and chops and superb seafood paella. And, even though it's not right on the water, you still can view stunning sunsets from its perch across the road from Eagle Beach. **Known for:** good selection of Spanish wines and homemade sangrias; excellent classic service; soft live guitar music and tiki torches make the setting very romantic. $ *Average main: $30 ⊠ La Cabana Beach Resort, J. E. Irausquin Blvd. 250, Eagle Beach* ☎ *297/520–1100* ⊕ *www.lacabana.com* ⊙ *Closed Sun.*

Mango's

$$$ | INTERNATIONAL | The main dining spot at Amsterdam Manor is a casual, alfresco affair that showcases international dishes and entertainment on a variety of theme nights. On those nights, specific cuisines, such as Italian or French, are highlighted, but it's the new Tuesday "Local Fishermen" night that's really pulling in the crowds. **Known for:** specialty themed buffets; congenial staff and festive atmosphere; interesting selection of "reef and ranch" combos for the less inquisitive. $ *Average main: $30* ⊠ *Amsterdam Manor Beach Resort, J. E. Irausquin Blvd. 252, Eagle Beach* ☎ *297/527–1100* ⊕ *www.mangos-restaurant-aruba.com.*

Matthew's Beachside Restaurant

$$ | INTERNATIONAL | The lively seaside eatery is popular with nonguests who make a special trip to enjoy great food (meats, fish, seafood, and a good selection of Italian specialties), superb sunsets, and the warm camaraderie of fun folks. It's a great place to catch the game or enjoy happy-hour specials and snacks, and they serve breakfast and lunch, too. **Known for:** all-you-can-eat-ribs Tuesday; Italian night Thursday; karaoke on the beach. $ *Average main: $25* ⊠ *Casa del Mar, J. E. Irausquin Blvd. 51, Eagle Beach* ☎ *297/588–7300* ⊕ *www.matthews-aruba.com.*

Passions on the Beach

$$$$ | INTERNATIONAL | Every night the weather allows, Amsterdam Manor Beach Resort transforms the area of Eagle Beach in front of the hotel into a magical, romantic, torchlit dining room. Imaginative creations are as beautiful as they are delicious, mostly "reef cuisine," as the main courses lean toward seafood, though meat lovers also are well indulged. **Known for:** signature seafood platters; creative cocktails; romantic toes-in-the-sand dining. $ *Average main: $45* ⊠ *Amsterdam Manor Beach Resort, J. E. Irausquin Blvd. 252, Eagle Beach* ☎ *800/969–2310* ⊕ *www. passions-restaurant-aruba.com.*

Red Fish

$$ | CARIBBEAN | The owners of the legendary downtown restaurant Driftwood and its sister operation Driftwood Fishing Charters opened this much smaller and far less formal dining nook centered around fresh fish and seafood. Locals love it and visitors are just beginning to discover it. **Known for:** authentic local experience; fresh fish and seafood by the pound; seafood pastas and paella. $ *Average main: $15* ⊠ *Orange Plaza, Italiestraat 50, Druif* ⊕ *On the road directly behind the Divi golf course* ☎ *297/280–6666* ⊕ *www.redfisharuba.com* ⊗ *Closed Sun., no dinner Mon.*

★ Screaming Eagle

$$$$ | INTERNATIONAL | Though diners may be initially lured to this elegant international eatery for the novel opportunity to dine in an actual bed, it's the exquisite culinary experiences created by award-winning chef Erwin that has them returning for more. The talent of the barkeeps has also garnered a loyal clientele, who are drawn to the classy lounge for creative cocktails. **Known for:** romantic dining in canopied lounge beds; rotating menu of seasonal specialties and three-course surprise menu also available in vegetarian and vegan versions; excellent wine cellar and multiple Wine Spectator awards. ⓈＡverage main: $45 ⊠ J. E. Irausquin Blvd. 228, Eagle Beach ☎ 297/587–8021 ⊕ www.screaming-eagle. net.

Tulip Caribbean Brasserie

$$ | INTERNATIONAL | This casual, partially alfresco almost-beach restaurant is across the street from the ocean, offering a global menu of dishes, including Indonesian, Jamaican, and French favorites. Service is fast and friendly, and the fare is reasonably priced and satisfying. **Known for:** authentic keshi yena, Aruba's national stuffed cheese dish; Dutch speciality snacks; large portions for good prices. Ⓢ Average main: $20 ⊠ MV Eagle Beach, J. E. Irausquin Blvd. 240, Eagle Beach ☎ ⊕ www.tulip-restaurant-aruba.com.

Twist of Flavors

$$$ | INTERNATIONAL | FAMILY | A glassed-in oasis in the Alhambra Mall offers big and tasty surprises on an eclectic menu that ranges from Dutch pancakes to burgers to Asian specialties to Caribbean-inspired seafood. Even better: everything is done exceedingly well. **Known for:** Sunday Caribbean seafood nights with a steel band; kaleidoscope of flavors from around the world; fun and friendly atmosphere. Ⓢ Average main: $30 ⊠ Alhambra Mall, J. E. Irausquin Blvd. 47, Druif ☎ 297/280–2518 ⊕ www. twistofflavorsaruba.weebly.com.

★ Windows on Aruba

$$$$ | INDONESIAN | This stylish, modern restaurant overlooking Divi Golf Village offers a contemporary American-influenced menu of primarily steak and seafood. Floor-to-ceiling windows surround the restaurant on all sides and look out onto both the sea and sunset as well as a two-story atrium. **Known for:** elegant prix-fixe Sunday brunch; seasonal menu specialties; porterhouse for two with chimichurri, portobello, and pepper sauce. Ⓢ Average main: $45 ⊠ Divi Village Golf Resort, J. E. Irausquin Blvd. 41, Druif ☎ 297/523–5017 ⊕ www.windowsonaruba.com.

Amsterdam Manor Beach Resort, a small hotel on Eagle Beach, is still family-run.

Hotels

The majority of hotels and resorts in this region were built to sprawl rather than tower, which is one reason why they call it the low-rise region. Most properties are no more than four stories tall, with Blue Residences as the exception. The Divi Resort family dominates the Druif Beach area with a collection of all-inclusives around their golf course.

Amsterdam Manor Beach Resort

$$$ | HOTEL | FAMILY | This intimate, family-run hotel offers excellent value without too many frills, right across the street from famed Eagle Beach. **Pros:** feels like a European village; friendly and helpful staff; all-inclusive option available. **Cons:** across the road from Eagle Beach; small pool; WaveRunners at beach can be noisy. ⑤ *Rooms from: $399* ⊠ *J. E. Irausquin Blvd. 252, Eagle Beach* ☎ *297/527–1100, 800/932–2310* ⊕ *www.amsterdammanor.com* 🛏 *72 rooms* ⑩ *No meals.*

Aruba Beach Club

$ | RESORT | FAMILY | The island's original time-share resort remains a favorite for families as well as those on a budget because of its larger suites that sleep up to six guests. **Pros:** family-friendly atmosphere with kiddie pool and playground; soft white-sand beach; good value. **Cons:** pool area can be very noisy; wave conditions can be dangerous for small children and poor swimmers; service is uninspired, except in the restaurant. ⑤ *Rooms from:*

$200 ✉ J. E. Irausquin Blvd. 51–53, Punta Brabo ☎ 297/524–3000 ⊕ www.arubabeachclub.net ⤴ 131 rooms ¶⦿¶ No meals.

Blue Residences

$$$ | HOTEL | Bookended by Aruba's two most famous beaches (Eagle and Palm) on its own private man-made sandy strand right across the street, the Blue Residence Towers—three columns of condo hotel-style suites ranging from one to five bedrooms—offer epic unfettered views of the sea. **Pros:** full concierge services; all rooms have great sea views; lovely infinity pool looks out on the sea. **Cons:** not directly on the beach; far walk to shopping; little on-site entertainment. ⑤ Rooms from: $350 ✉ J. E. Irausquin Blvd. 26, Eagle Beach ☎ 297/525–3600 ⊕ www.bluearuba.com ⤴ 120 room ¶⦿¶ No meals ☞ 3-night min.

Bubali Bliss Studios

$ | HOTEL | Secreted behind Super Food, this economical and chic option is within walking distance of famed Eagle Beach, with beautifully decorated rooms (all of which have modern kitchens) and an inviting oasis pool surrounded by studios, deluxe studios, and one-bedroom apartments that are ideal for extended stays. **Pros:** flexible anytime self-check-in and check-out; pool garden area with hammocks; free Wi-Fi. **Cons:** not on a beach; three-night minimum stay requirement; no on-site dining. ⑤ Rooms from: $205 ✉ Bubali 147, Eagle Beach ☎ 297/587–5262 ⊕ www.bubalibliss.com ⤴ 10 rooms ¶⦿¶ No meals ☞ 3-night min.

★ Bucuti & Tara Beach Resort

$$$$ | HOTEL | Having achieved the first carbon-neutral status in the Caribbean in 2018, and also often voted one of the most romantic hotels in the Caribbean, this landmark adults-only luxury boutique hotel offers exquisite personal service in an extraordinary beach setting. **Pros:** eco-friendly barefoot luxury at its best; unique arrival experience with personal concierge and iPad check in; accessible management, with owners often on property. **Cons:** a little too quiet for some (no nighttime entertainment); not all rooms have sea views; no longer doing beach weddings. ⑤ Rooms from: $583 ✉ L. G. Smith Blvd. 55B, Druif ☎ 297/583–1100 ⊕ www.bucuti.com ⤴ 104 rooms ¶⦿¶ Free Breakfast.

Casa del Mar Beach Resort

$ | RESORT | FAMILY | The one- and two-bedroom suites at this beachside time-share resort are quite comfortable though not overly luxe, but they come with fully equipped kitchens, and the resort, which sits on a white-sand beach, offers a wide range of amenities like tennis courts and a gym and services like water sports and a kids' program. **Pros:** home-away-from-home feeling; family-friendly. **Cons:** pool area can get crowded; rooms feel a bit

The beachfront at Bucuti & Tara Beach Resorts

dated; few quiet spots on property; strong strong current and quick drop-off can be dangerous for small children and poor swimmers. ⑤ *Rooms from: $225* ⊠ *L. G. Smith Blvd. 53, Eagle Beach* ☎ *297/582–7000* ⊕ *www.casadelmar-aruba.com* ⇆ *147 suites* ⦿ *No meals.*

Costa Linda Beach Resort
$$ | RESORT | FAMILY | Operating like a small village unto itself, this all-suites, four-story, horseshoe-shaped time-share resort provides an ideal environment for families, with a kids' pool and colorful beachfront playground. **Pros:** spacious fully equipped suites; many activities available on-site; great beach. **Cons:** not all rooms have sea views; can get noisy when kids are everywhere; some rooms are outdated and there is no nightlife. ⑤ *Rooms from: $343* ⊠ *J. E. Irausquin Blvd. 59, Eagle Beach* ☎ *297/583–8000* ⊕ *www. costalinda-aruba.com* ⇆ *155 rooms* ⦿ *No meals.*

★ Divi Aruba All-Inclusive
$$$$ | RESORT | FAMILY | The more upscale choice of Divi's sister all-inclusives, which share the same gorgeous stretch of Druif Beach, has a 60-room tower addition with more modern rooms and four super-luxe two-bedroom oceanfront suites with whirlpool tubs. **Pros:** on wonderful stretch of beach with family-friendly surf; kids under 12 stay free; cosmopolitan lively vibe. **Cons:** older rooms are small by modern standards; not all rooms have sea views; reservations mandatory for the more upscale restaurants. ⑤ *Rooms from: $508* ⊠ *L. G. Smith Blvd. 93, Druif*

☎ *297/525–5200, 800/554–2008* ⊕ *www.diviaruba.com* ⮡ *269 rooms* ○| *All-inclusive* ☞ *3- or 5-night min.*

Divi Dutch Village Beach Resort

$$$ | **HOTEL** | **FAMILY** | This modern all-suites resort, renovated top to bottom in 2017, features very spacious, fully equipped accommodations ideal for families wishing to cook their own meals, but they now also offer an all-inclusive option that gives access to all the food and drink at both Divi Aruba and the Tamarijn. **Pros:** family-friendly; spacious suites fully equipped with modern appliances; supermarkets are within walking distance. **Cons:** not directly on the beach; no ocean views from most rooms; no nightly entertainment unless you go to sister resorts. $ *Rooms from: $403* ✉ *J. E. Irausquin Blvd. 47, Druif* ☎ *297/583–5000, 800/367–3484* ⊕ *www. dividutchvillage.com* ⮡ *123 rooms* ○| *No meals.*

Divi Village Golf & Beach Resort

$$$ | **RESORT** | **FAMILY** | All the rooms at this all-suites resort community across the street from Druif Beach include fully equipped kitchens, but the all-inclusive option is also available. **Pros:** excellent golf course; dedicated beach space with lounge chairs and shade palapas across the street; lush and lovely grounds with freshwater lagoons and wildlife. **Cons:** no suites have two beds, only one bed and a sleeper sofa; the resort is not beachfront; no ocean-view rooms. $ *Rooms from: $435* ✉ *J. E. Irausquin Blvd. 93, Druif* ☎ *297/583–5000* ⊕ *www.divivillage.com* ⮡ *250 suites* ○| *All-inclusive* ☞ *3-night min.*

★ La Cabana Beach Resort & Casino

$ | **RESORT** | **FAMILY** | A warm and friendly complex of mostly time-share units draws repeat visitors (primarily families) who enjoy the spacious accommodations equipped with everything you could possibly need for a home base away from home, including a fully equipped kitchen. **Pros:** lively family-friendly atmosphere with large pool facilities; the only on-resort chapel on the island; laundry facilities on every floor. **Cons:** you must cross the road to get to the beach; limited number of shade palapas; few rooms have sea views. $ *Rooms from: $222* ✉ *J. E. Irausquin Blvd. 250, Eagle Beach* ☎ *297/520–1100* ⊕ *www.lacabana.com* ⮡ *449 rooms* ○| *Free Breakfast.*

Manchebo Beach Resort & Spa

$$ | **RESORT** | One of the original landmark low-rise resorts built on Aruba has refreshed and reinvented itself over the past few years to become a dedicated health and wellness resort with daily complimentary seafront yoga, Pilates classes, and healthy and healing cuisine menus. **Pros:** on the island's broadest and most pristine white-sand beach; all-inclusive meal plans available; great on-site restaurants and culinary events. **Cons:** rooms are on the small side; not much in way of entertainment; not all rooms have sea views. $ *Rooms from: $385* ⊠ *J. E. Irausquin Blvd. 55, Druif* ☎ *297/582–3444, 800/223–1108* ⊕ *www.manchebo.com* ⇴ *72 rooms* ⦿ *Free Breakfast.*

MVC Eagle Beach

$ | HOTEL | A tiny budget boutique hotel across the road from a very quiet portion of beautiful Eagle Beach, this is your best bet for a no-frills, clean and comfortable stay at a good price. **Pros:** unbeatable price; free Wi-Fi; friendly and helpful staff. **Cons:** lacks all the amenities of larger resorts; not for those who want to be away from children; across the street from the beach. $ *Rooms from: $250* ⊠ *J. E. Irausquin Blvd. 240, Eagle Beach* ☎ *297/587–0110* ⊕ *www.mvceaglebeach.com* ⇴ *19 rooms* ⦿ *No meals.*

Tamarijn Aruba All-Inclusive Beach Resort

$$$$ | RESORT | FAMILY | One of Aruba's original and most popular family-friendly all-inclusives—and a sister resort to the Divi Aruba—spans a gorgeous quarter-mile stretch of Druif Beach and offers access to the entire shared complex of bars, restaurants, and services. **Pros:** complimentary shuttle service between Divi resorts and the Alhambra Casino and Mall; recently refreshed lobby and food outlets; all rooms are oceanfront. **Cons:** rooms are small by modern standards; no room service; main pool can be crowded. $ *Rooms from: $550* ⊠ *J. E. Irausquin Blvd. 41, Punta Brabo* ☎ *297/594–7888, 800/554–2008* ⊕ *www.tamarijnaruba. com* ⇴ *236 rooms* ⦿ *All-inclusive* ⚐ *3-night min.*

Nightlife

Most of the nightlife in this area revolves around the resorts where there are often special shows and live music for guests around pool areas, and some of their beach bars have regular special events like karaoke nights (the public is usually welcome).

BARS

★ Fusions Wine and Tapas Piano Bar

PIANO BARS/LOUNGES | This classy lounge in the Alhambra Mall is an ideal spot to grab a glass of wine, a tasty bite, or a steak grilled on a Big Green Egg, the outdoor ceramic charcoal grill. There's usually soft, live piano music and a solo singer. Patrons often stop by before or after gambling at the big casino next door. Fusions is owned by the Divi group, so guests at those resorts should check with their concierge for special savings. ⊠ *Alhambra Mall, Druif* ☎ *297/280–9994* ⊕ *www.fusion-aruba.com.*

Rock 'N' Rock Bar

BARS/PUBS | It might be only rock and roll but they love it at this friendly little rock music spot. In fact, it's all they play! Live and DJ-driven rock music from all decades and all genres are played, and a great beer menu draws the fans to hear the local bands. ⊠ *Caya Taratata 15 L-3, Pos Abao* ☎ *297/730–0987* ⊕ *www.rockn-rockaruba.com.*

Shopping

This region isn't known for great shopping, though all the resorts have their own little stores and the area has the island's largest supermarkets—good to know if you're self-catering.

FOOD

Kong Hing Supercentre

CONVENIENCE/GENERAL STORES | This clean, orderly supermarket within easy walking distance of Druif Beach stocks all the typical grocery store staples, including fresh produce, meats, canned goods, baked goods, and a wide selection of beer, wine, and liquor. ⊠ *L. G. Smith Blvd. 152, Druif* ☎ *297/583–0892* ⊕ *www. konghingaruba.com.*

★ SuperFood Plaza

FOOD/CANDY | This massive emporium offers all kinds of extras; it's more like a small department store. Beyond a huge fresh produce section, fresh fish and seafood market, bakery, and deli section, there's also a café, a drugstore, and even a toy store on-site. It's truly a one-stop for all your needs. ⊠ *Bubali 141-A, Eagle Beach* ☎ *297/522–2000* ⊕ *www.superfoodaruba.com.*

MALLS AND MARKETPLACES

★ The Shops at Alhambra Mall

CLOTHING | There's an eclectic array of shops and dining in alfresco Alhambra Mall with the casino as its focal point. Dotted with small retail stores and souvenir shops and a full-service market and deli, the mall also has multiple fast-food outlets as well as finer dining options like Fusions Wine & Tapas Bar, We'r Cuba, and Twist of Flavors. There's often live music at night, and there's a small spa. Stores are open late, but the casino is open until the wee hours. ⊠ *L. G. Smith Blvd. 47, Druif* ⊕ *www.diviresorts.com.*

SPAS

Indulgence by the Sea Spa

SPA/BEAUTY | The spa-salon serving Divi Aruba and Tamarijn all-inclusives offers a wide range of premium services. Begin your journey to relaxation with a rose-filled pure essential oil footbath, cold cucumbers for the eyes, and a lavender heat wrap. Products are organic and natural—all handpicked and tested by the owner. The spa portion is at Divi Aruba, and the salon that specializes in bridal parties for special-occasion hair and makeup is at Tamarijn. They also service Divi Dutch Village and Divi Golf Village. ✉ *J. E. Irausquin Blvd. 45, Druif* ☎ *297/583–0083* ⊕ *spaaruba.com.*

Purun Spa

SPA/BEAUTY | Reflecting the kind of upscale elegance and high-quality services one would expect of a spa located in adults-only luxury boutique Bucuti & Tara Beach Resort, this oasis of pampering offers a wide range of unique treatments with a focus on natural products and holistic health and wellness. There's even an outdoor cabana for massages and services. It's open to the public, but reservation preferences are given to resort guests. ✉ *Bucuti & Tara Beach Resort, L. G. Smith Blvd. 55B, Eagle Beach* ☎ *297/583–1100* ⊕ *www.purunspa.com.*

★ Spa del Sol

SPA/BEAUTY | An ideal Zen sanctuary right on the sea—and a partner to Manchebo resort's extensive health, wellness, and yoga services and retreats—this Balinese-themed spa right on the sea hosts a bevy of partly open-air treatment rooms so you can hear the relaxing sounds of the waves; they even have hot tubs on the beach. A full range of treatments is available, including couple's massages. ✉ *Manchebo Beach Resort, J. E. Irausquin Blvd. 55* ☎ *297/582–6145* ⊕ *www.spadelsol.com.*

PALM BEACH AND NOORD AND WESTERN TIP (CALIFORNIA DUNES)

Updated by
Sue Campbell

⦿ Sights	🍴 Restaurants	🛏 Hotels	🛍 Shopping	🍸 Nightlife
★★★★☆	★★★★☆	★★★★☆	★★★★☆	★★★★☆

NEIGHBORHOOD SNAPSHOT

TOP EXPERIENCES

■ **Swim, Stroll, and People-Watch:** Explore the island's liveliest stretch of sand and sea unfettered by barriers or barricades.

■ **Water Sports Galore:** Partake in a wide assortment of water sports available along Palm Beach.

■ **Electric Tropical Nights:** The Palm Beach "strip" is full of bars, restaurants, cafés, malls, and shops.

■ **High Seas Adventures:** Climb aboard a cool watercraft for an afternoon (or day) of snorkeling, sunset viewing, or partying.

■ **Go Casino-Hopping:** The high-rise hotels are stacked side by side, and most have their own glitzy casino, so you can hop from one to another, without the use of a car.

■ **Visit the Western Tip:** Climb the historic California lighthouse and explore the cool sand dunes surrounding it.

GETTING HERE AND AROUND

Depending on traffic, it's about a 20- to 25-minute drive from the airport to the Palm Beach/Noord area, which is an approximately 7-mile drive straight along L. G. Smith Boulevard, one of Aruba's main thoroughfares. There is plenty of free parking around the high-rise hotels and beach area, as well as paid lots. There is no public bus service directly from the airport, but there are public buses from the downtown Oranjestad main Arubus terminal that stop at every major resort. Shared transport vans and private transfer options are available, as are taxis.

QUICK BITES

■ **Dushi Bagels & Burgers.** Grab a "beach bag to go" of the island's best assorted bagels, as well as bagel sandwiches, wraps, and gourmet burgers. ⊠ *Playa Linda Beach Resort, Irausquin Blvd. 87, Palm Beach* ⊕ *dushibagelsandburgers.com*

■ **Eduardo's Beach Shack.** This cheery little hut is famous for their healthy and delicious fresh fruit and veggie juices, smoothies, bowls, and creative vegan options. ⊠ *J. E. Irausquin Blvd. 87, Noord*

■ **Scott's Brats.** The expat American owners brought a taste of a home to their alfresco Palm Beach bar with authentic Wisconsin brats and sausages and Chicago-style hot dogs, and they have funnel cakes. ⊠ *J. E. Irausquin Blvd. 87, Palm Beach* ⊕ *scottsbratsaruba.weebly.com*

Soft white sand for miles, clear aqua surf, lively beach bars, exciting water sports, fine dining, world-class casinos, superb shopping, electric nightlife, first-rate resorts—it's all within a stone's throw in Palm Beach. So park your car and get ready to pleasure-hop your way through Aruba's liveliest beach region, no matter the time of day.

Palm Beach and Noord

The district of Noord is home to the strip of high-rise hotels and casinos that line Palm Beach. The hotels and restaurants, ranging from haute cuisine to fast food, are densely packed into a few miles running along the beachfront. When other areas of Aruba are shutting down for the night, this area is guaranteed to still be buzzing with activity. Don't be afraid to venture outside of the tourism epicenter, though, because pristine wild coastal scenes and charming local neighborhoods await.

◉ Sights

Bubali Bird Sanctuary
BODY OF WATER | More than 80 species of migratory birds nest in this man-made wetland area inland from the island's strip of high-rise hotels. Herons, egrets, cormorants, coots, gulls, skimmers, terns, and ducks are among the winged wonders in and around the two interconnected artificial lakes that make up the sanctuary. Perch up on the wooden observation tower for great photo ops. ✉ *J. E. Irausquin Blvd., Noord* 🎫 *Free.*

★ Butterfly Farm
FARM/RANCH | **FAMILY** | Hundreds of butterflies and moths from around the world flutter about this spectacular garden. Guided tours (included in the price of admission) provide an entertaining look into the life cycle of these insects, from egg to caterpillar to chrysalis to butterfly or moth. After your initial visit, you can return as often as you like for free during your vacation. ■ **TIP→ Go early in the morning when the butterflies are most active; wear bright colors**

KEY	
1	*Exploring Sights*
1	*Restaurants*
1	*Hotels*

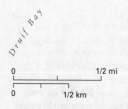

Druif Bay

0   1/2 mi

0   1/2 km

Eagle Beach

J.E. Irausquin Blvd.

Manchebo Beach

Divi Village

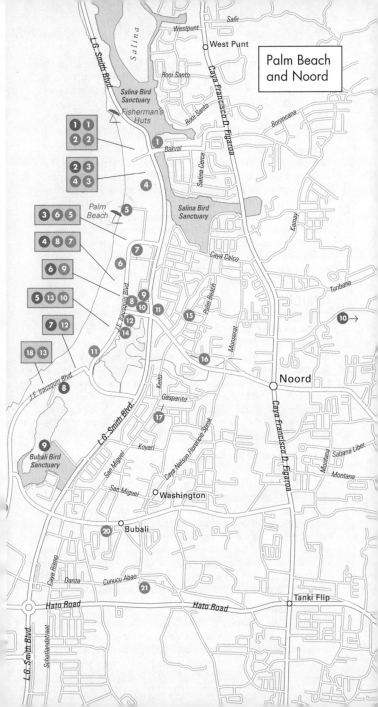

Palm Beach and Noord

Salina

Safir

Westpunt

West Punt

Rooi Santo

Caya Francisco D. Figaroa

Rooi Santo

Salina Cerca

Boroncana

Salina Bird
Sanctuary

Fisherman's
Huts

1 **1**
2 **2**

1 Bakval

2 **3**
4 **3**

4

Palm
Beach

5

Salina Bird
Sanctuary

Caya Calco

Kanay

3 **6** **5**

4 **8** **7**

7

Palm Beach

Turibana

6 **9**

6

9

8

5 **13** **10**

10

11

15

10 →

J.E. Irausquin Blvd.

7 **12**

12

14

Monserat

18 **13**

11

16

J.E. Irausquin Blvd.

8

Keito

Noord

Caya Francisco D. Figaroa

9

Bubali Bird
Sanctuary

Gasparito

17

L.G. Smith Blvd.

Koyari

San Miguel

Caya Nelson Florencio Sprok

Montana

Sabana Liber

Montana

San Miguel

Washington

20 Bubali

Caya Ritmo

Danza

Cunucu Abao

21

Montana

Hato Road

Hato Road

Tanki Flip

L.G. Smith Blvd.

Scholandstraat

if you want them to land on you. Early morning is also when you are most likely to see the caterpillars emerge from their cocoons and transform into butterflies or moths. A small café out front serves healthy light drinks and snacks. ☒ *J. E. Irausquin Blvd., across from Divi Phoenix Aruba Beach Resort, Palm Beach* ☏ *297/586–3656* ⊕ *www.thebutterflyfarm.com* ☑ *$15 (good for return visits).*

★ Philip's Animal Garden

FARM/RANCH | FAMILY | This nonprofit exotic animal rescue and rehabilitation foundation is a wonderful, child-friendly attraction you'll find just off the beaten track up in Noord. Each guest is given a bag of treats for the animal residents, which include monkeys, peacocks, an emu, an ocelot, an alpaca, and many other types of creatures you're not likely to see elsewhere on Aruba. There's a large playground and ranch so little ones can run. It is also a stop on some tours. ☒ *Alto Vista 116, Noord* ☏ *297/593–5363* ⊕ *www. philipsanimalgarden.com* ☑ *$10.*

Casinos

The Casino Aruba

CASINO—SIGHT | Well refreshed since the Hilton took over the Radisson in 2005, and renamed the Casino Aruba, you'll still find the famous starry skies on the casino ceiling, but there are upgraded machines and the latest digital games; it's open until 3 am. Poker is often the game of choice here with a dedicated Poker Room that has 10 tables, large-screen TVs, and frequent tournaments. ☒ *J. E. Irausquin Blvd. 81, Palm Beach* ☏ *297/526–6930* ⊕ *www.tcaruba.com.*

★ The Casino at the Ritz-Carlton

CASINO—SIGHT | A very "ritzy" casino just off the lobby of the Ritz-Carlton Aruba offers many traditional table games like blackjack, craps, roulette, Caribbean stud poker, baccarat, and Texas hold 'em and more than 300 snazzy modern slots: spinning reels, video reels, and video games with jackpots available 24/7. Tables run from 6 pm to 3 am. They also have two sports-betting kiosks and offer "luxury" bingo several times a week. Points accumulated from their VIP casino club card can be used toward hotel extras like dining, spa treatments, and room nights. ☒ *L. G. Smith Blvd. 107, Palm Beach* ☏ *297/527–2222* ⊕ *www.ritzcarlton.com.*

Excelsior Casino

CASINO—SIGHT | Located in the Holiday Inn Aruba Resort, this is one of the oldest casinos on the island, and unfortunately its age is beginning to show; it stays open until 4 am. Many sections in the common areas are somewhat run-down and the air-filtering

Good-Luck Charms

Arubans take myths and superstitions very seriously. They flinch if a black butterfly flits into their home, because this symbolizes death. And on New Year's Eve they toss the first sips of whiskey, rum, or champagne from the first bottle that's opened in the New Year out the door of their house to show respect to those who have died and to wish luck on others. It's no surprise, then, that good-luck charms are part of Aruba's casino culture as well.

The island's most common good-luck charm is the *djucu* (pronounced *joo*-koo), a brown-and-black stone that comes from the sea and becomes hot when rubbed. It's often called the "lucky nut." Many people have them put in gold settings—with their initials engraved in the metal—and wear them around their necks on a chain with other charms such as an anchor or a cross. Another item that's thought to bring good luck is a small bag of sand. The older generation of women might wear them tucked discreetly into their bras.

system could use an upgrade, but there is still a good selection of standard slots, blackjack, craps, and roulette tables, and the place is usually hopping with locals for daily bingo games. The blackjack tables are known for not hitting "the soft 17." ⊠ *Holiday Inn Resort Aruba, J. E. Irausquin Blvd. 230, Palm Beach* ☎ *297/586–7777* ⊕ *www.excelsiorcasino.com.*

Hyatt Regency Casino
CASINO—SIGHT | This spacious, modern casino has 13 gaming tables, 221 slot machines, and great live music (Tuesday to Sunday); it stays open until 4 am. First-time customers get a $10 credit for joining the Players Advantage Club. The bar serves signature drinks and hand-rolled cigars. ⊠ *Hyatt Regency Aruba Beach Resort & Casino, J. E. Irausquin Blvd. 85, Palm Beach* ☎ *297/586–1234* ⊕ *www.hyatt.com.*

Liv Casino
CASINO—SIGHT | A small but welcoming little casino is just off the lobby of Barcelo Aruba Resort. It's a great spot to try your luck at some brand-new slot games. There are also some interesting promotions every week and it's open until 3 am. ⊠ *Barcelo Aruba Resort, J. E. Irausquin Blvd. 82, Palm Beach* ☎ *297/ 280–4000* ⊕ *www.liv-casino.com.*

Orchid Casino

CASINO—SIGHT | This lively casino is also popular with locals for blackjack, roulette, craps, Caribbean poker, and baccarat; those are in addition to some 300 slot machines. The vibe is fresh and modern. With 12 gaming tables and more live poker games than anywhere else on the island, it's your best bet if you are looking for the weekly poker tournament. A Sports and Race Book is also on-site. It's open until 4 am. ⊠ *Riu Palace Antillas, J. E. Irausquin Blvd. 77, Palm Beach* ☎ *297/525–7777.*

★ Stellaris Casino

CASINO—SIGHT | This is one of the largest casinos on the island, and it's open 24/7. There are 500 modern interactive slots as well as 26 tables with games like craps, roulette, poker, and blackjack. There's a state-of-the-art race and sports-betting operation. Don't forget to join the VIP Club program, where you can earn points, comps, and prizes. They offer free cocktails for gamers, and there are many special theme and entertainment nights. ⊠ *Aruba Marriott Resort, L. G. Smith Blvd. 101, Palm Beach* ☎ *297/586–9000* ⊕ *www.stellariscasino.com.*

 Beaches

Fisherman's Huts (*Hadicurari*)

BEACH—SIGHT | Beside the Ritz-Carlton, Fisherman's Huts is a windsurfer's and kiteboarder's haven. Swimmers might have a hard time avoiding all the boards going by, as this is the nexus of where the lessons take place for both sports, and it's always awash in students and experts and board hobbyists. It's a gorgeous spot to just sit and watch the sails on the sea, and lately it's become increasingly popular among paddleboarders and sea kayakers, too. Only drinks and small snacks are available at the operator's shacks. There are no restrooms, but the Ritz lobby is nearby in a pinch. **Amenities:** food and drink; parking (free); water sports. **Best for:** windsurfing. ⊠ *Palm Beach* ✛ *North of Aruba Marriott Resort.*

★ Palm Beach

BEACH—SIGHT | This is the island's most populated and popular beach running along the high-rise resorts, and it's crammed with every kind of water-sports activity and food-and-drink emporium imaginable. It's always crowded no matter the season, but it's a great place for people-watching, sunbathing, swimming, and partying; and there are always activities happening like paddle-boarding, and even paddleboard yoga. The water is pond-calm; the sand, powder-fine. **Amenities:** food and drink; showers; toilets;

water sports. **Best for:** partiers; swimming. ⊠ *J. E. Irausquin Blvd. between Divi Phoenix Resort and Ritz-Carlton Aruba, Palm Beach.*

Restaurants

Aqua Grill

$$$$ | SEAFOOD | Aficionados flock here to enjoy a wide selection of seafood and fish in a New England–style decor. Dishes like smoked swordfish and grilled red snapper served with a mango salsa are top of the list, and they also nod to a New England feel with Maine lobster. **Known for:** daily fresh seafood, either from local fishermen or flown in; massive raw bar; consistently high-quality specials. ⑤ *Average main: $32* ⊠ *J. E. Irausquin Blvd. 374, Palm Beach* ☎ *297/586–5900* ⊕ *www.aqua-grill.com.*

Atardi

$$$$ | INTERNATIONAL | This rollicking beach bar by day morphs into a surprisingly romantic pop-up, toes-in-the-sand dining spot as soon as the sun begins to set—the sunsets rarely disappoint. Fresh fish and seafood are the specialty but meat lovers will be well sated with the excellent filet mignon and short ribs dishes. **Known for:** torchlit, seaside dining; attentive personal service; excellent fish and seafood. ⑤ *Average main: $40* ⊠ *Aruba Marriott Resort, L. G. Smith Blvd. 101, Palm Beach* ☎ *297/520–6537* ⊕ *www.marriott.com.*

Azia Restaurant Lounge

$$$ | ASIAN FUSION | Secreted away just off the main Palm Beach strip, seek out the hidden Buddha to find the twinkling lights that lead to an absolutely enchanting upscale Asian-fusion emporium with stunning decor and Aruba's longest bar. Enjoy an eclectic selection of dim sum, sushi, and creative meat and seafood dishes that can be paired with sake, Japanese beer, and whiskey, or a killer handcrafted cocktail from their expert mixologists. **Known for:** great place for groups as it seats 350 and serves excellent shareables; VIP semiprivate room for up to 12 people is unique to the island; the adjacent alfresco Zen Garden lounge has hot music and late-night bites. ⑤ *Average main: $30* ⊠ *J. E. Irausquin Blvd. 348, Palm Beach* ⊹ *Across the street from the Hilton* ☎ *297/586–0088* ⊕ *www.giannisgroup.com/azia.*

Bavaria Food & Beer

$$ | GERMAN | A variety of German beers, schnitzel, and bratwurst presented in a true beer-hall setting are guaranteed to provide that Oktoberfest feeling. The hearty cuisine is paired with over 20 different types of beer by owners who take their imbibing seriously. **Known for:** German cuisine served in an "oom-pa-pa" atmosphere;

fun and friendly crowd of locals and visitors; outdoor beer garden suitable for large groups. $ *Average main: $25 ⊠ Palm Beach 186, Noord ☎ 297/586–8550 ⊕ www.bavaria-aruba.com ۞ Closed Sun.*

BLT Steak

$$$$ | AMERICAN | Though this restaurant in the Ritz-Carlton is designed to replicate a New York–style steak house, the stellar sunset views are unmistakably Caribbean. The chef is a master at meat, and his daily blackboard specials can't help but be inspired by the bounty of the sea, so pescatarians will always be just as happy as carnivores; there's even a kids' menu. **Known for:** 28-day, dry-aged porterhouse for two; surprisingly good selection of oysters and seafood platters; three-course prix-fixe "date night" menu (choice of duck, beef, or fish). $ *Average main: $55 ⊠ Ritz-Carlton Aruba, L. G. Smith Blvd. 107, Palm Beach ☎ 297/527–2222 ⊕ www.ritzcarlton.com.*

Casa Nonna

$$$$ | ITALIAN | FAMILY | The breakfast spot known as Solanio takes on a whole new identity in the evenings as it transforms into Casa Nonna, dedicated to serving up authentic Italian cuisine. The prix-fixe four-course menu focuses on specific regions of Italy on a rotating basis, and the house-made desserts are divine. **Known for:** authentic house-made pastas and sauces; Mediterranean comfort food, sometimes with a fusion twist; top-quality cured meats and cheeses. $ *Average main: $35 ⊠ Ritz-Carlton Aruba, L. G. Smith Blvd. 107, Noord ☎ 297/527–2222 ⊕ casanonna.com/aruba.*

★ Da Vinci Ristorante

$$$$ | ITALIAN | FAMILY | Don't let the rustic decor fool you: this is not your average Italian resort eatery, though it's an inviting choice for large groups. Da Vinci pulls out all the stops to present a seriously upscale, authentic, and creative menu of Mediterranean favorites. **Known for:** creative Italian fare such as crab-and-lobster cannelloni; excellent wine cellar; family-friendly atmosphere. $ *Average main: $35 ⊠ Holiday Inn Resort Aruba, J. E. Irausquin Blvd. 230, Palm Beach ☎ 297/586–3600 ⊕ www.holidayarubaresort.com/en-us/ da-vinci-ristorante ۞ Closed Wed. and Sat.*

Gasparito Restaurant & Art Gallery

$$$ | CARIBBEAN | This enchanting hideaway can be found in a beautifully restored 200-year-old *cunucu* (country) house, where you can dine indoors or out. Aruban specialties including *keshi yena* and Gasparito chicken (with brandy, white wine, pineapple, and four secret ingredients) are on the menu, the latter with a sauce passed down through the owner's family. **Known for:** a unique country-house setting that is part art gallery; time-honored Aruban specialties; very limited seatings with required reservations.

⑤ *Average main: $28* ⊠ *Gasparito 3, Noord* ☎ *297/594–2550*
⊕ *www.gasparito.com* ☾ *Closed Sun.*

Hostaria Da' Vittorio

$$$ | ITALIAN | At one of Aruba's most celebrated Italian eateries, part of the fun at this family-oriented spot is watching chef Vittorio Muscariello prepare authentic Italian regional specialties in his open kitchen. The staff helps you choose wines from the extensive list and recommends portions of hot and cold antipasti, risottos, and pastas. ⑤ *Average main: $28* ⊠ *L. G. Smith Blvd. 380, Palm Beach* ☎ *297/586–3838* ⊕ *www.hostariavittorio.com.*

Madame Janette

$$$$ | EUROPEAN | The food at this rustic restaurant, named after the Scotch bonnet pepper called Madame Janette in Aruba, is surprisingly not Caribbean spicy, but French-inspired from the classically trained chef. Though many dishes are infused with Caribbean flavors, especially fish and seafood, you'll find a lot of classic sauces served with the meats. **Known for:** top-quality meat and seafood; craft beers and even a beer sommelier; specials that focus on local seasonal ingredients. ⑤ *Average main: $35* ⊠ *Cunucu Abao 37, Cunucu Abao* ☎ *297/587–0184* ⊕ *www.madamejanette.info* ☾ *Closed Sun. No lunch.*

★ Melt Away Cafe

$$$ | INTERNATIONAL | Situated in the lovely colonial courtyard of Paseo Hernencia affording great views of the nightly water and light show, this new little nook serves up gourmet grilled cheese, small bites like killer crostini, and everything fondue and raclette one could imagine. After 6 pm, they also serve some comprehensive international mains like sea bass topped with Gouda, as well as vegan options. **Known for:** a wide variety of shareable fondue and raclette options; creative offerings of sandwiches and salads for lunch; decadent desserts like chocolate fondue and sweet ravioli with dulce de leche ice cream. ⑤ *Average main: $25* ⊠ *Paseo Herencia, J. E. Irausquin Blvd. 382, Palm Beach* ☎ *297/280–0044* ⊕ *meltawayaruba.com* ☾ *No lunch weekends.*

MooMba Beach Bar & Restaurant

$$$ | INTERNATIONAL | Best known as a beach party spot, this legendary hangout also has very good food. Dinner under the giant palapa is first-rate, as is lunch—particularly since it's the perfect place for people-watching along Aruba's busiest beach. **Known for:** massive all-you-can-eat barbecue buffet on Friday and Sunday; catch of the day topped in signature sauce; 1-pound racks of honey-glazed ribs. ⑤ *Average main: $30* ⊠ *J. E. Irausquin Blvd. 230, Palm Beach* ☎ *297/586–5365* ⊕ *www.moombabeach.com.*

Jumbo shrimp are a delicious staple at Madame Janette.

Old Cunucu House

$$$ | CARIBBEAN | Since the mid-1990s executive chef Ligia Maria has delighted diners with delicious and authentic *crioyo* (local) cuisine in a rustic and cozy traditional cunucu house. Try the house version of Aruba's famous keshi yena—chicken, raisins, olives, cashews, peppers, and rice in a hollowed-out Gouda rind—or thick, hearty *stobas* (stews) of goat or beef. **Known for:** secret family recipes of traditional Aruban cuisine; hearty portions and good prices; family-run and family-friendly atmosphere. ⑤ *Average main: $23* ✉ *Palm Beach 150, Palm Beach* ☎ *297/586–1666* ⊕ *www.theoldcunucuhouse.com.*

Papillon

$$$$ | FRENCH | The jailhouse theme may take you aback (it's inspired by the famous Devil's Island prisoner Henri Charrière), but the popular landmark spot on the strip will win you over with its delicious French-Caribbean fusion cuisine. The menu includes both classics like frogs' legs, escargots, and French onion soup as well as duck with passion-fruit sauce and local snapper with grilled shrimp and a creole sauce. **Known for:** classic French old-school cuisine with a slight Caribbean twist; bargain-priced, early-bird prix-fixe menu; rotating monthly themed specials. ⑤ *Average main: $35* ✉ *J. E. Irausquin Blvd. 348A, Palm Beach* ☎ *297/586–5400* ⊕ *www.papillonaruba.com.*

★ pureocean

$$$ | CONTEMPORARY | Unfettered sea views and stellar sunsets with tiki lights and lit-up palms make pureocean the signature

dining spot of Divi Aruba Phoenix. The menu offers continental
favorites with a Caribbean twist, and guests can enjoy fish, steak,
and seafood beachside in the bistro or with toes in the sand mere
steps from the sea. **Known for:** romantic seaside dinners; a wide
selection of international fare; shareable apps and small plates like
quinoa shrimp fritters. $ *Average main: $30 ⊠ Divi Aruba Phoenix
Beach Resort, J. E. Irausquin Blvd. 75, Palm Beach* ☎ *297/586–
6066* ⊕ *www.pureoceanrestaurant.com.*

★ Quinta del Carmen

$$$$ | DUTCH | Quinta del Carmen is set in a beautifully restored
100-year-old mansion with stunning manicured lawns and a lovely
outdoor courtyard. The cuisine here is best defined as modern
Caribbean-Dutch with a few traditional Dutch favorites, like
cheese croquettes and mushrooms and cream, appearing on the
menu as "Grandma's favorites." The watermelon salad is sweet,
salty, and perfectly refreshing, and the *sucade-lappen* (flank steak
stewed in red wine and herbs) has a depth of flavor that comes
from hours in the pot. **Known for:** upscale Dutch comfort food; creative seafood like shrimp piña colada; gorgeous antique mansion
setting full of avant-garde art. $ *Average main: $40 ⊠ Bubali 119
Aruba, Noord* ☎ *297/587–7200* ⊕ *www.quintadelcarmen.com.*

Ruinas del Mar

$$$$ | CARIBBEAN | This scenic spot is famous for its gorgeous
circuit of waterfalls cascading around stone "ruins" that offers
the ideal setting for romantic dinners. Specialties include stone-
hearth-cooked items from around the world. **Known for:** lavish
Sunday champagne brunch; theme nights including Land & Sea
Mondays, Lobster Wednesdays, and Wine Saturdays; the resident
black swans. $ *Average main: $42 ⊠ Hyatt Regency Aruba
Beach Resort and Casino, J. E. Irausquin Blvd. 85, Palm Beach*
☎ *297/586–1234* ⊕ *aruba.hyatt.com* ☽ *No lunch. No dinner Sun.*

Ruth's Chris Steak House

$$$$ | AMERICAN | This American steak house chain has been a pop-
ular fixture of the Aruba Marriott for years and continues to draw
locals and visitors in droves. It is a no-nonsense carnivore's delight
with the focus on top-quality steak; those looking for something
else will find a few interesting seafood specialties like Louisi-
ana-style barbecue shrimp and sizzling blue crab cakes. **Known for:**
top-quailty prime beef; famous dipping trio for steaks: black truffle
butter, shiitake demi-glace, and honey soy glaze; chopped salad
with bacon, eggs, lemon basil dressing, and crispy onions. $ *Aver-
age main: $45 ⊠ Aruba Marriott Resort and Stellaris Casino, L. G.
Smith Blvd. 103, Palm Beach* ☎ *297/520–6600* ⊕ *www.ruthschris.
com* ☽ *No lunch.*

Sunset Grille

$$$$ | **INTERNATIONAL** | Simple and elegant, without a lot of extra gimmicks, this is a no-nonsense modern steak and seafood spot with a focus on fresh and locally sourced ingredients whenever possible. Though there's air-conditioned seating inside, grab a seat outside for dinner to find out why this is called the Sunset Grille. **Known for:** the signature chocolate souffle with coconut crust and vanilla ice cream; rotating prix-fixe chef's choice menu for two; tender wood-grilled highly marbled steaks. ⑤ *Average main: $40* ✉ *Hilton Aruba, J. E. Irausquin Blvd. 81, Noord* ☎ *297/586–6555* ⊕ *www.hilton.com.*

2 Fools and a Bull

$$$$ | **INTERNATIONAL** | Enjoy an intimate evening of culinary entertainment that plays like a fun dinner party with friends rather than something you pay for. At most, 16 guests are assembled around the U-shaped communal dinner table for a five-and-a-half course culinary adventure. **Known for:** an intimate chef's table experience; perfect wine pairings (optional); adults-only with reservations required far in advance. ⑤ *Average main: $110* ✉ *Palm Beach 17, Noord* ☎ *297/586–7177* ⊕ *www.2foolsandabull.com* ⊙ *Closed weekends.*

Hotels

Aruba Marriott Resort & Stellaris Casino

$$$$ | **RESORT** | **FAMILY** | This full-service resort offers both family-friendly amenities as well as an adults-only luxury floor with its own pool and bar. **Pros:** inviting full-service spa and beauty salon; calm, kid-friendly surf out front; one of the best 24/7casinos on the island. **Cons:** main pool can be noisy and crowded with kids; not all rooms have sea views; beachfront can become crowded in high season. ⑤ *Rooms from: $605* ✉ *L. G. Smith Blvd. 101, Palm Beach* ☎ *297/586–9000, 800/223–6388* ⊕ *www.marriott.com* ⇥ *414 rooms* ⦿ *No meals.*

Barcelo Aruba

$$$$ | **RESORT** | **FAMILY** | This family-friendly all-inclusive offers something for everyone, with an extensive pool complex, great nightly entertainment, a dedicated kids' club, and an eclectic choice of à la carte dining. **Pros:** spacious rooms, many with good sea views; excellent location for Palm Beach water sports and shopping; Royal Club level has a dedicated dining room and lounge. **Cons:** beach can get very crowded; pool area can be very noisy with activities; difficult to get a shaded lounge on the beach if you don't snag one early morning. ⑤ *Rooms from: $720* ✉ *J. E. Irausquin Blvd. 83,*

Palm Beach ☎ *297/586–4500* ⊕ *www.barcelo.com* ↩ *373 rooms* ⊙ *All-inclusive.*

★ Boardwalk Small Hotel Aruba

$$$ | **HOTEL** | A gorgeous and luxurious boutique tropical oasis right across the street from Palm Beach, this family-run gem offers a collection of newly refreshed casita-style rooms that surround an inviting pool. **Pros:** beautiful grounds and decor close to Palm Beach; dedicated beach space with chair service and shade palapas; intimate resort feel with many secret oasis spots. **Cons:** not right on the beach; no housekeeping or concierge services on Sunday; no restaurant on-site but room service breakfast is available. ⑤ *Rooms from: $435* ⊠ *Bakval 20, Palm Beach* ☎ *297/586–6654* ⊕ *www.boardwalkaruba.com* ↩ *46 units* ⊙ *No meals.*

Brickell Bay Beach Club & Spa Boutique Hotel

$ | **HOTEL** | Right in the heart of the main tourist street behind the high-rise resort Palm Beach strip is this adults-only urban stay with its own hidden pool and courtyard. **Pros:** resort has a small spa on-site; free Wi-Fi and calls to North America; dedicated space on Palm Beach with free shuttle. **Cons:** noisy, busy area; no ocean views; busy pool. ⑤ *Rooms from: $200* ⊠ *J. E. Irausquin Blvd. 370, Palm Beach* ☎ *297/586–0900* ⊕ *www.brickellbayaruba.com* ↩ *98 rooms* ⊙ *Free Breakfast.*

★ Divi Aruba Phoenix Beach Resort

$$$$ | **RESORT** | **FAMILY** | With incredible views from its high-rise tower, stunning rooms awash in tropical colors and state-of-the-art amenities, and comfortable, homey accommodations, Divi Aruba Phoenix rises above the fray on busy Palm Beach. **Pros:** beautifully appointed rooms, some with whirlpool bathtubs; great private beach away from the main Palm Beach frenzy; all units have sea views. **Cons:** no shuttle service to other Divi properties; no all-inclusive plan; no reserving shade palapas. ⑤ *Rooms from: $489* ⊠ *J. E. Irausquin Blvd. 75, Palm Beach* ☎ *297/586–1170* ⊕ *www. diviarubaphoenix.com* ↩ *240 rooms* ⊙ *Free Breakfast.*

Hilton Aruba Caribbean Resort and Casino

$$$$ | **HOTEL** | **FAMILY** | Following a takeover by the Radisson in 2015, the iconic Hilton Aruba offers a new look while still retaining the best of its traditional allure and upscale experiences for all ages. **Pros:** excellent beachfront area never feels crowded, even when at capacity; grand ballroom is ideal for big events; Palm Beach Club VIP program has special perks and its own lounge. **Cons:** not all rooms have sea views; long lines at the breakfast buffets; food and drink can be pricey. ⑤ *Rooms from: $770* ⊠ *J. E. Irausquin Blvd. 81, Palm Beach* ☎ *297/586–6555* ⊕ *www.hiltonaruba.com* ↩ *357 rooms* ⊙ *No meals.*

The Aruba Marriott Resort & Stellaris Casino is in the heart of Palm Beach.

★ Holiday Inn Resort Aruba

$$$$ | **RESORT** | **FAMILY** | The resort's massive lemon-yellow buildings that sprawl across a prime spot on Palm Beach offer a revelation compared to what most might think a Holiday Inn stay might entail, offering inviting rooms, a fun vibe, and distinct sections that will appeal to those looking for quiet active fun, or a family-friendly environment. **Pros:** thematic zones provide distinct amenities; kids eat and stay free and enjoy an excellent stand-alone kids' club; excellent on-site dining can include an all-inclusive meal plan. **Cons:** not all rooms have sea views; the casino (not owned by the resort) needs updating; reception is frequently busy with big groups. $ *Rooms from: $480* ⊠ *J. E. Irausquin Blvd. 230, Palm Beach* ☎ *297/586–3600, 800/465–4329* ⊕ *www.holidayarubaresort.com* 🛏 *603 rooms* ¶◯¶ *All-inclusive.*

Hotel Riu Palace Antillas

$$$$ | **RESORT** | Right next door to Hotel Riu Palace Aruba, its family-friendly sister, this high-rise tower is strictly for adults, offering all-inclusive rates and a fabulous pool area right on the beach as well as stellar sea views from many rooms. **Pros:** full bottles of standard spirits, beer, and soft drinks in all rooms; arguably the best and biggest all-inclusive buffet on the island; 24/7 room service included; only adults 18 and over. **Cons:** rooms are small by modern standards; common areas appear more corporate than resort-tropical; not all rooms have a sea view. $ *Rooms from: $600* ⊠ *J. E. Irausquin Blvd. 77, Palm Beach* ☎ *297/ 526–4100* ⊕ *www.riu.com* 🛏 *481 rooms* ¶◯¶ *All-inclusive.*

Hotel Riu Palace Aruba

$$$$ | RESORT | FAMILY | This family-friendly all-inclusive is a massive complex surrounding an expansive water circuit leading to the sea with a choice of five restaurants and offering scads of free activities. **Pros:** spacious water circuit for families; a wide choice of entertainment and dining; nice shallow beachfront. **Cons:** beach and pool area get very busy and noisy; few spots to escape in solitude; few rooms have unobstructed sea views. $ *Rooms from: $600 ⊠ J. E. Irausquin Blvd. 79, Palm Beach ☎ 297/ 586–3900 ⊕ www.riu.com ⇨ 400 rooms* ☉ *All-inclusive.*

Hyatt Regency Aruba Resort Spa and Casino

$$$ | RESORT | Located on 12 acres of magnificent beachfront, this landmark resort, famous for its faux ruins and waterfalls that flow into a koi pond, offers both a chic stay for couples and a friendly setting for families. **Pros:** guest rooms include the Hyatt's signature Grand Bed; lush tropical landscaping leads down to spacious beachfront; many rooms have spectacular ocean views. **Cons:** main pool area can be noisy with children; some standard rooms are on the small side with small balconies; not all rooms have sea views. $ *Rooms from: $450 ⊠ J. E. Irausquin Blvd. 85, Palm Beach ☎ 297/586–1234, 800/554–9288 ⊕ www.hyatt.com ⇨ 359 rooms* ☉ *Free Breakfast.*

Marriott's Aruba Ocean Club

$$$$ | RENTAL | FAMILY | First-rate amenities and lavishly decorated villas with balconies and full kitchens have made this time-share an island favorite. **Pros:** relaxed atmosphere; feels more like a home than a hotel room; excellent beach. **Cons:** beach can get crowded; attracts large families, so lots of kids are about; grounds are not in sea view. $ *Rooms from: $500 ⊠ L. G. Smith Blvd. 99, Palm Beach ☎ 297/586–2641 ⊕ www.marriott.com ⇨ 206 rooms* ☉ *No meals.*

Playa Linda Beach Resort

$$$ | RESORT | FAMILY | Looking something like a stepped Mayan pyramid—the design maximizes sea views from the balconies—this older time-share hotel also has a homey feel, with full kitchens in all the spacious units. **Pros:** great beach location; spacious rooms and townhomes; lots of distractions for the kids. **Cons:** not all rooms are of the same standard; can be a crowded and busy beachfront; not all rooms have sea views. $ *Rooms from: $450 ⊠ J. E. Irausquin Blvd. 87, Palm Beach ☎ 297/586–1000 ⊕ www. playalinda.com ⇨ 144 rooms, 3 townhomes* ☉ *No meals.*

Ritz-Carlton, Aruba

$$$$ | HOTEL | Bookending the long string of resorts along famed Palm Beach, this massive hotel sits on a broad stretch of white sand with all rooms overlooking the sea. **Pros:** exemplary personal service including beach servers on Segways; spacious grounds so it never feels crowded; stunning sunset views from all rooms and the two-story atrium lobby bar. **Cons:** sheer size and design gives it a big-box feel; attracts many large groups; pricey for standard rooms compared to others of similar quality on the same beach. ⑤ *Rooms from: $1,500* ✉ *L. G. Smith Blvd. 107, Palm Beach* ☎ *527–2222* ⊕ *www.ritzcarlton.com/en/hotels/caribbean/aruba* 🛏 *320 rooms* ⑩ *No meals.*

 # Nightlife

The 2-mile stretch of road in front of the high-rise resorts called The Strip is where you'll find most of the nightlife action in Palm Beach, though there are also some pubs and clubs worth seeking out in the surrounding areas of Noord. The clubs tend to come and go, but The Strip is always chock-full of opportunities to let loose after the sun goes down in the area's squares, courtyards, and outdoor malls, and threaded throughout are vendor kiosks. You can easily barhop on foot to find the vibe that suits you best by following the music that suits you best. If you're staying in a Palm Beach resort, there's no need for a car or taxi.

BARS
★ Bugaloe Bar & Grill

BARS/PUBS | Night and day, this crazy colorful beach bar at the tip of De Palm Pier on busy Palm Beach is hopping and bopping with visitors and locals alike. Paint-spattered wooden tables and chairs on a plank floor under a massive palapa draw barefoot beach-combers in for frozen cocktails, cold beer, and casual fare where live music is king. The revelry starts as early as happy hour and continues well into the evening. Karaoke nights, salsa nights, and even a crazy fish night on Monday: there's always something wild and fun going on there. It's also an optimal spot to catch a magical sunset over the waves. There's free Wi-Fi, too. ✉ *De Palm Pier, J. E. Irausquin Blvd. 79, De Palm Pier, Palm Beach* ☎ *297/586–2233* ⊕ *www.bugaloe.com.*

Craft

BARS/PUBS | Right on the strip, this cool little café bar is the ideal spot for a pre- or post-party drink and some good people-watching. There's an excellent signature cocktail list, as well as gourmet coffees, craft beers, and interesting bites. Next door, their sister property, Lola, opens at night for taco specials with matching margaritas. ✉ *J. E. Irausquin Blvd. 348-A, Palm Beach* ☎ *297/586–6999.*

The Great Room Lobby Bar

PIANO BARS/LOUNGES | Easy-listening local bands get the party started at the Aruba Marriott's lobby bar. It's a classy venue and an ideal spot for before- or after-dinner drinks. And the bartenders take their creative mixology seriously, even competing in bartending competitions. Superb signature cocktails are what you come for. ⊠ *Aruba Marriott Resort & Stellaris Casino, L. G. Smith Blvd. 101, Palm Beach* 🕾 *297/586–9000* ⊕ *www.marriott.com.*

★ Gusto

DANCE CLUBS | Definitely Aruba's most cosmopolitan high-octane dance club, Gusto is where master bartenders show off excellent flair skills while serving up fabulous cocktails to pretty people who want to party late into the night. The island's hottest DJs and a dazzling light show keep the dancing going nonstop. Late-night happy hour is from 9 pm to 11 pm. All kinds of special events and theme nights add to Gusto's allure as a highly popular party spot. VIP bottle service is available, too. ⊠ *J. E. Irausquin Blvd. 348-A, Palm Beach* 🕾 *297/592–8772* ⊕ *www.gustoaruba.com* ⊙ *Closed Mon.*

★ Hard Rock Cafe Aruba

MUSIC CLUBS | This classic rock-branded bar and restaurant has anchored the nightlife scene along The Strip since 2008. You'll find live bands on a big outdoor stage cresting a massive terrace. You can come for a burger or other hearty fare, or just stand outside and enjoy the show. ⊠ *South Beach Bldg., Palm Beach 55, Palm Beach* 🕾 *297/586–9966* ⊕ *www.hardrockcafe.com.*

★ Lobby Bar and Restaurant

BARS/PUBS | Though they do serve dinner, this spot has more of a chic supper club lounge vibe than a dining room, and later in the evening it morphs into an upscale nightclub. Catering to an older, cosmopolitan crowd, there's an excellent wine list, and a choice of indoor or outdoor seating. Live music or a DJ sets the scene depending on the night and the hour, and after 11 pm there's a strict over-21 policy. ⊠ *J. E. Irausquin Blvd. 348, Palm Beach* 🕾 *297/280–5330* ⊕ *www.lobbyaruba.com.*

Local Store

BARS/PUBS | Contrary to its name, it's not a store but a bar, and a very local one at that. Live local bands, lots of resident partiers, and a laid-back, down-to-earth atmosphere make this the place to kick back and have fun, especially on weekends. Good prices on drinks, local beer, craft beers, and local Aruban snacks like funchi fries (made from seasoned cornmeal or polenta with a crispy outside and a creamy inside) and over a dozen kinds of artisanal chicken wings attract the tourists, too. ✉ *Palm Beach 13A, Noord* ☏ *297/586–1414* ⊕ *www.localstorearuba.com.*

★ MooMba Beach Bar

BARS/PUBS | As the central party spot on the busiest part of Palm Beach, this open-air bar is famous for its Sunday-night blowouts with big crowds of locals gathering to dance in the sand to live bands or DJs. The barkeeps are flair and mixology masters, and happy hours are very hot. You'll find both early and late drink specials every night except Sunday. The attached restaurant is also a wonderful surf-side spot for breakfast, lunch, and dinner. There's free Wi-Fi and public outdoor bucket showers are a bonus. ✉ *J. E. Irausquin Blvd. 230, Palm Beach* ⊹ *Between Holiday Inn and Marriott Surf Club* ☏ *297/586–5365* ⊕ *www.moombabeach.com.*

★ purebeach

BARS/PUBS | South Beach–style cocktails and tapas are served in this bar and restaurant in the Divi Phoenix Aruba Resort. It's got a cool, hip vibe, offering couches in the sand surf-side, which are lit by tiki torches at night; some kind of live music is often on the menu, too. It's an ideal place to kick off the night for a sunset happy hour cocktail or snack. Specials events include a Wednesday night Burger Bash ($3 off burgers, $3 Balashi draft beer, $4 house cocktails) and Thursday Mojito Day ($4 mojitos all day). ✉ *Divi Phoenix Aruba Resort, J. E. Irausquin Blvd. 75, Palm Beach* ☏ *297/586–6606* ⊕ *www.purebeacharuba.com.*

★ Sopranos Piano Bar

PIANO BARS/LOUNGES | With a theme loosely based on the famous HBO TV series, Sopranos has a fun atmosphere, and live piano nightly encourages the crowd to join in a sing-along. Top-notch barkeeps shake up a big list of creative cocktails, and the top-shelf spirit list is impressive. It's loud and rowdy most nights, but nostalgic and low-key when there are no crowds. A DJ sometimes spins late into the night on weekends. ✉ *Arawak Garden Mall, L. G. Smith Blvd. 177, Palm Beach* ☏ *297/586–8622* ⊕ *www.sopranospianobararuba.com.*

South Beach

DANCE CLUBS | It might not be located on a beach, but you can expect a South Beach Miami vibe with electronic music, flashy lights, and a big outdoor dance floor with DJs. The party starts late and gets crazier as it gets later, attracting a young hip crowd with bottle service and different special events every night of the week as well as the island's longest happy hour (5–11 pm). ✉ *55D Palm Beach, Noord* ⊹ *Just off the strip across from the Hilton (follow your ears)* ☏ *297/586–9838* ⊕ *www.southbeacharuba.com.*

📖 Shopping

CIGARS
★ Aruhiba Cigars
TOBACCO | Look for the big red windmill just off Palm Beach to find this little factory kiosk outlet where the owner hand-rolls quality cigars from tobacco grown on Aruba. Aruhibas have become as popular as Cubans with locals on the island, and in terms of quality they are seriously on par with those from Havana. They are also a legal option for visitors seeking cigars to bring back to the United States. ⊠ *Historic Red Windmill, J. E. Irausquin Blvd. 330* ☎ *297/567–1599.*

Captian Jack Liquor & Cigars
SPECIALTY STORES | This store specializes in a wide selection of quality liquors and cigars. ⊠ *La Hacienda Mall, J. E. Irausquin Blvd. 382, Palm Beach* ☎ *297/280–1142* ⊕ *captian-jack-aruba-liquor-cigar-wine.business.site.*

CLOTHING AND ACCESSORIES
★ The Lazy Lizard
CLOTHING | Fun and trendy beachwear and resort fashions along with accessories like fancy flip-flops, sandals, Aruba-inspired T-shirts, and totes for the whole family are sold here. There are souvenirs as well. A sister store in the Alhambra Mall is part of The Salamander Group, which donates a portion of proceeds to local charities. ⊠ *South Beach Centre, Palm Beach 55, Palm Beach* ⊹ *Next to the Hard Rock Cafe* ☎ *297/592–7805* ⊕ *www.thelazylizard.com.*

GIFTS AND SOUVENIRS
★ The Juggling Fish
CLOTHING | This whimsical shop just off the sand is really two separate entities. One side is Juggling Fish Swimwear, a comprehensive selection of quality bathing suits and beach accessories for the entire family, and the other side is dedicated to a panopoly of creative and unique gifts and souvenirs including avant-garde jewelry and handcrafted items. The staff is warm and friendly, and a portion of all proceeds goes to community programs and charities. ⊠ *Playa Linda Beach Resort, Palm Beach* ☎ *297/592–7842* ⊕ *www.thejugglingfish.com.*

★ T. H. Palm & Company
ANTIQUES/COLLECTIBLES | With an eclectic collection of upscale and exclusive items curated from all over the world by the owner, this unique boutique offers everything from top-line fashions for men and women, including footwear, handcrafted jewelry, and accessories, to art deco items for the home and novelty gifts for

pets. It's a very popular spot for locals to buy gifts as well as for visitors to buy one-of-a-kind souvenirs. A portion of all proceeds goes to the community through a special give-back program. ⊠ *J. E. Irausquin Blvd. 87, Palm Beach* ☎ *297/ 598–7804* ⊕ *www. thpalmandcompany.com.*

JEWELRY
★ Shiva's Gold and Gems

JEWELRY/ACCESSORIES | A reputable family-run business with shops throughout the Caribbean, this Palm Beach Plaza location saves shoppers from heading to Oranjestad for the type of top-quality diamonds and jewelry downtown is famous for (though there is a location downtown as well). Luxury watches, precious gems, gold, silver, and more are first-rate here, and this is the only store on Aruba that belongs to the Leading Jewelers of the World, which has fewer than 100 retail members. ⊠ *Palm Beach Plaza, L. G. Smith 95, Palm Beach* ☎ *297/586–2586* ⊕ *www.shivasjew-elers.com.*

MALLS AND MARKETPLACES
The Cove Mall

SHOPPING CENTERS/MALLS | Though billed as a shopping mall, this brand-new complex is more of a dining and nightlife emporium than a shopping spot. With apartment rentals on top, the bottom level has filled with an abundance of trendy cafés and restaurants including Italian, Mexican, Asian, French, Caribbean, and gourmet burgers. There's also a popular Colombian nightclub and a cool little craft beer brewery bar. ⊠ *J. E. Irausquin Blvd. 384 A, Unit 5, Palm Beach* ⊹ *Across the street from Holiday Inn* ☎ *297/744–9194.*

★ Palm Beach Plaza

SHOPPING CENTERS/MALLS | Aruba's most modern multistory mall has three floors of shops offering fashion, tech, electronics, jewelry, souvenirs, and more. Entertainment includes, glow-in-the-dark bowling, a modern video arcade, a sports bar, and the main floor indoor courtyard is often used for local festivals and events like fashion shows. Dining includes a food court and lots of stand-alone restaurants and bars, and there are also modern air-conditioned cinemas and a spa within. Free Wi-Fi and parking is a bonus, too. ⊠ *L. G. Smith Blvd. 95, Palm Beach* ☎ *297/586–0045* ⊕ *www.palmbeachplaza.com.*

★ Paseo Herencia

SHOPPING CENTERS/MALLS | **FAMILY** | A gorgeous, old-fashioned colonial-style courtyard and clock tower encases souvenir and specialty shops, cinemas, dining spots, cafés, and bars in this low-rise alfresco mall just off Palm Beach, famous for its "liquid fireworks" shows when three times a night neon-lit water fountains waltz to music in a choreographed dance. Visitors can enjoy it for free from an outdoor amphitheater where many cultural events take place, and there's an Aruban walk of fame there. There's also a fancy carousel for children. A must-visit—if not for the shopping, then for the water show. ✉ *J. E. Irausquin Blvd. 382, Palm Beach* ☎ *297/586–6533* ⊕ *www.paseoherencia.com.*

PERFUMES AND COSMETICS
★ Maggy's Perfumery and Salon
PERFUME/COSMETICS | A true local success story, this is one of the four locations in a local chain that began as a small salon in San Nicolas and evolved into a major perfumery with salons and stores. Though the original Maggy has since passed, the business she began in 1969 is still going strong with her daughter at the helm and many family members still running the business. Quality perfumes and beauty products, as well as health and beauty care services are all to be found at all outlets. ✉ *Paseo Herencia, L. G. Smith Blvd. 382, Palm Beach* ☎ *297/ 529–2118* ⊕ *www.maggys-aruba.com.*

SPAS
★ Eforea Spa
SPA/BEAUTY | Hilton's answer to Zen incarnate, the soothing white seafront building beckons you to enter a world of relaxing signature "journeys" in a Japanese-inspired enclave. Treatments include both the typical and avant-garde, and there are options for both women and men, as well as special seaside massages for couples. There's also a stellar water circuit and full-service beauty salon on-site. ✉ *Hilton Aruba Resort, J. E. Irausquin Blvd. 81, Palm Beach* ☎ *297/526–6052* ⊕ *www.hiltonaruba.com.*

Island Yoga
SPA/BEAUTY | This little Zen oasis may not be a spa in the traditional sense, but it's definitely centered around health and wellness for the mind, body, and spirit. Founded by Rachel Brathen, an internationally known yoga teacher, speaker, and author, there are classes for all skill levels including yoga-on-paddleboard lessons and multiday retreats. Nourish, the on-site café, serves healthy snacks and drinks, and there's also a shop with yoga attire and accessories. ✉ *Noord 19-A, Noord* ☎ *297/280–0025* ⊕ *www. islandyoga.com.*

Mandara Spa
SPA/BEAUTY | Aruba Marriott's Mandara Spa was created along a Balinese theme and offers specialty Indonesian-style treatments that incorporate the *boreh* (a traditional warm healing pack of special spices) followed by an Aruba-inspired wrap using local aloe

Many Aruba resorts have thier own spas providing body treatments and massages.

and cucumber. The menu also lists a wide variety of skin and body treatments for both women and men, and there's a full-service hair and nail salon, ideal for a wedding party. Honeymooners and couples will appreciate special packages that include private couple's treatment rooms, extra-large whirlpool baths, and Vichy showers. ✉ *Aruba Marriott Resort & Stellaris Casino, L. G. Smith Blvd. 101, Palm Beach* ☎ *297/520–6750* ⊕ *www.mandaraspa.com/spa/Aruba-Marriott-Resort-and-Aruba-Ocean-Club.aspx.*

New Image Spa

SPA/BEAUTY | A full-service spa and beauty center in the Barcelo Resort offers a comprehensive range of services. Beyond the typical spa menu of massages, facials, wraps, and mani-pedis, you can also get foot reflexology, detoxification, permanent makeup, cosmetology, hair removal, injectables, or simple hairdressing. The concept of all treatments is to utilize organic and natural products whenever possible. ✉ *Barcelo Resort, J. E. Irausquin Blvd. 83, Palm Beach* ☎ *297/586–4500* ⊕ *www.newimagearuba.com.*

★ Pure Indulgence Spa

SPA/BEAUTY | Divi Aruba Phoenix's glassed-in multilevel spa has the island's only sea view mani-pedi treatment room—a pretty unique feature. Another unique feature is the Pure Couple's Escape that includes massage and time spent in the private Lover's Suite with Jacuzzi baths, a steam room, and premium Hansgrohe rain showers. ✉ *Divi Phoenix Aruba Beach Resort, J. E. Irausquin Blvd. 75, Palm Beach* ☎ *297/586–6606* ⊕ *www.purespaaruba.com.*

★ The Ritz-Carlton Spa

SPA/BEAUTY | Natural elements are the main theme at this upscale spa, which has 13 treatment rooms and an adjoining fitness center with daily classes, including yoga and personal trainers, as well as a soothing indoor water therapy pool. Signature treatments feature local island ingredients like aloe, divi-divi tree oil, and local coffee (for scrubs), and there's a good selection of treatments for men. ⊠ *Ritz-Carlton Aruba, L. G. Smith Blvd. 107, Palm Beach* ☎ *297/527–2525* ⊕ *www.ritzcarlton.com.*

ZoiA Spa

SPA/BEAUTY | It's all about indulgence at the Hyatt's upscale spa, named after the Papiamento word for balance. Gentle music and the scent of botanicals make the world back home fade into the background. Newly arrived visitors to the island can opt for the jet-lag massage that combines reflexology and aromatherapy while couples may enjoy the Serenity package for two that includes champagne and massage. There's even a mother-to-be package available. Island brides can avail themselves of a full menu of beauty services ranging from botanical facials (using local ingredients) to a full makeup job for the big day. ⊠ *Hyatt Regency Aruba Beach Resort & Casino, J. E. Irausquin Blvd. 85, Palm Beach* ☎ *297/586–1234* ⊕ *www.hyatt.com.*

Western Tip (California Dunes)

No trip to Aruba is complete without a visit to the California Lighthouse, and it's also worth exploring the rugged area of the island's western tip. This is the transition point between Aruba's calmer and rougher coasts. Malmok Beach and Arashi Beach are popular with locals and excellent spots for grabbing dramatic sunset photos.

Sights

★ Alto Vista Chapel

BUILDING | Meaning "high view," Alto Vista was built in 1750 as the island's first Roman Catholic Church. The simple yellow and orange structure stands out in bright contrast to its stark desert-like surroundings, and its elevated location affords a wonderful panoramic view of the northwest coast. Restored in 1953, it still holds regular services today and also serves as the culmination point of the annual walk of the cross at Easter. You will see small signposts guiding the faithful to the Stations of the Cross all along the winding road to its entrance. This landmark is a typical stop on most island tours. ■ **TIP→ Make sure to buy coconut water from the famous coconut man out front.** ⊠ *Alto Vista Rd., Noord* ✛ *Follow the rough, winding dirt road that loops around the island's northern tip, or from the hotel strip, take Palm Beach Rd. through three intersections and watch for the asphalt road to the left.*

★ California Lighthouse

LIGHTHOUSE | FAMILY | Built in 1910, the landmark lighthouse on the island's eastern tip is open to the public, and visitors can climb the spiral stairs to discover a fabulous panoramic view. Declared a national monument in 2015, the lighthouse was named after the merchant ship *Californian,* which sunk nearby, the tragedy that inspired its construction. ⊠ *2 Hudishibana, Westpunt* ☎ *297/699–0995* 💲 *$5.*

 Beaches

★ Arashi Beach

BEACH—SIGHT | This is the local favorite, a half-mile stretch of gleaming white sand with a rolling surf and great snorkeling. It can get busy on weekends—especially on Sunday—with local families bringing their own picnics, but during the week it is typically quiet. Lately, however, more visitors have been discovering it since some tours and sports outfitters now stop here for kayaking and snorkeling. ■ **TIP→ There's a $1 fee to use the toilets. Amenities:** food and drink; toilets; parking (free). **Best for:** swimming; snorkeling; walking. ⊠ *Malmokweg* ✛ *West of Malmok Beach, on the west end.*

Boca Catalina

BEACH—SIGHT | A fairly isolated strip off a residential area, this tiny white-sand cove attracts snorkelers with its shallow water filled with fish and cool little caves. Swimmers will also appreciate the calm conditions. There aren't any facilities nearby, a few public shade palapas but no chairs, however, so pack provisions and your own snorkel gear. It's popular with locals on weekends. **Amenities:** none. **Best for:** snorkeling; swimming. ⊠ *Malmokweg* ✛ *Between Arashi Beach and Malmok Beach, north of intersection of Rtes. IB and 2B.*

Malmok Beach (*Boca Catalina*)

BEACH—SIGHT | On the northwestern shore, this small, nondescript beach borders shallow waters that stretch 300 yards from shore. There are no snack or refreshment stands, but shade is available under the thatched umbrellas. Right off the coast here is a favorite haunt for divers and snorkelers—the wreck of the German ship *Antilla,* scuttled in 1940. All the snorkel boat tours stop here for a

Alto Vista Chapel, on the windy northwest coast of Aruba, was built in 1750.

dip as well. There is no easy access into the water from the shore; it's very rocky with sharp cliffs and steep descents. Snorkeling is best done from a boat. **Amenities:** none. **Best for:** solitude; snorkeling; sunsets. ⊠ *J. E. Irausquin Blvd., Malmokweg.*

🍴 Restaurants

Faro Blanco

$$$$ | **ITALIAN** | Next to the iconic California lighthouse in the former lighthouse-keeper's home, this restaurant is best known for its upscale Italian fare and grand open-air terrace overlooking the rugged west coast seascape. The restaurant is open all day, but it's renowned for sunset views, when reservations are a must. **Known for:** stunning sunset views; classics like osso buco and calamari; filetto alla trattoria steak topped with red wine, brown sugar, cloves, cinnamon, sliced oranges, and fresh strawberries. Ⓢ *Average main: $35* ⊠ *California Lighthouse* ☎ *297/586–0786* ⊕ *www.faroblancorestaurant.com.*

The Restaurant at Tierra del Sol

$$$$ | **INTERNATIONAL** | The main restaurant at Tierra del Sol sits next to the cliff-top pool and golf course and offers great views of the northwest coast and the California lighthouse. Breakfast and lunch offer a creative selection of fare, but it's the inspired all-you-can-eat mix-and-match tapas dinner menu that draws folks for a lovely sunset experience. **Known for:** great views and romantic candle-light alfresco dining; popular à la carte Sunday brunch; prix-fixe "all u can taste" menu with dozens of apps, tapas, and add-ons.

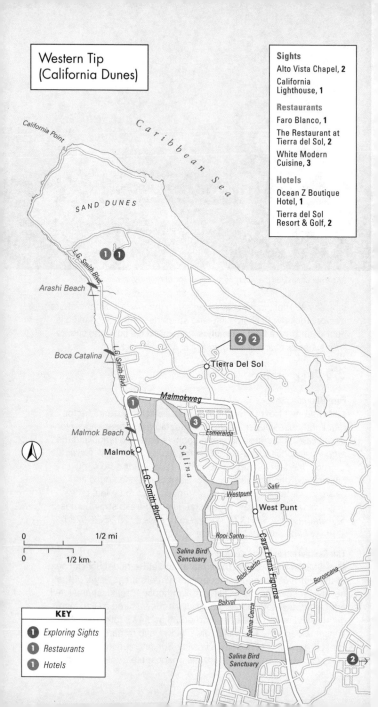

Western Tip (California Dunes)

Sights
Alto Vista Chapel, **2**
California Lighthouse, **1**

Restaurants
Faro Blanco, **1**
The Restaurant at Tierra del Sol, **2**
White Modern Cuisine, **3**

Hotels
Ocean Z Boutique Hotel, **1**
Tierra del Sol Resort & Golf, **2**

California Point

Caribbean Sea

SAND DUNES

L.G. Smith Blvd.

Arashi Beach

Boca Catalina

Tierra Del Sol

Malmokweg

Malmok Beach

Malmok

Esmeralda

Salina

Safir

Westpunt

West Punt

Cava Frans Figaroa

Rooi Santo

0   1/2 mi
0   1/2 km

Salina Bird Sanctuary

Robi Santo

Salina Garza

Boroncana

Bakval

Salina Bird Sanctuary

KEY

1 *Exploring Sights*
1 *Restaurants*
1 *Hotels*

$ Average main: $65 ⊠ Tierra del Sol Resort ☎ 297/586–7800 ⊕ www.tierradelsol.com ☾ No dinner Sun. and Mon.

★ White Modern Cuisine

$$$$ | FUSION | Celebrated local chef Urvin Croes was one of the very first to introduce the concept of molecular gastronomy to this island, and his penchant for deconstructing elements and experimenting with food chemistry and flavors is rivaled only by his talent for artistic plating. This unique dining spot overlooking the pool at the luxe Gold Coast Estates Clubhouse provides a perfect setting of indoor and outdoor dining for those seeking to try his avant-garde creations as well as his take on traditional dishes like Aruban stew and Chilean sea bass. **Known for:** small-plates menu that encourages grazing and sharing; gourmet brunch; prix-fixe surprise menu, with or without wine pairings. $ Average main: $40 ⊠ Gold Coast Estates, Diamante 300 ☎ 297/280–2800 ⊕ www.whitecuisine.com.

 # Hotels

Ocean Z Boutique Hotel

$$$$ | HOTEL | A unique luxury boutique resort far from the touristy fray is across the road from the wild and scenic Malmok Cliffs, offering rooms surrounding a solarium pool as well as a few oceanfront suites. **Pros:** chic solitary escape away from the crowds; gorgeous scenic setting with sea views; intimate and personal first-rate service. **Cons:** not within walking distance to any other dining or shopping; not on a beach; no entertainment. $ Rooms from: $490 ⊠ L. G. Smith Blvd. 526, Malmokweg ☎ 297/586–9500 ⊕ www.oceanzaruba.com ⤴ 13 rooms ❀ Free Breakfast.

Tierra del Sol Resort & Golf

$$$$ | RESORT | More of a sprawling gated community than a resort, these upscale properties range in size from two-bedroom condos and duplex villas to sprawling home-style abodes with pools and manicured lawns, making it the choice of many a visiting celebrity. **Pros:** complimentary transportation to Arashi Beach close by; high level of personalized services available; exclusive private-club vibe. **Cons:** far from shopping and nightlife; limited choice of dining; not directly on a beach. $ Rooms from: $600 ⊠ Tierra Del Sol, Caya di Solo 10, Noord ☎ 297/439–8578 ⊕ www.tierradelsol.com ⤴ 10 condos, 10 villas ❀ No meals.

🛍 Shopping

There is little shopping on this far end of the island beyond small boutiques in the hotels and the terrific Spa at Tierra del Sol.

SPAS
★ The Spa at Tierra del Sol

SPA/BEAUTY | Expect high-end massages, wraps, scrubs, and skin treatments, and a full hair- and nail-care salon at at Tierra del Sol's luxury spa. Highlights include the sea-sand detox skin treatment or the private whirlpool where couples can relax with champagne in peace. Spa guests are welcome to use the fitness center and lounge by the cliff-side pool looking out at the California Lighthouse. ⊠ *Tierra del Sol, Caya di Solo 10, Noord* ☎ *297/ 586–7800* ⊕ *www.tierradelsol.com.*

SAN NICOLAS AND SAVANETA

Updated by
Sue Campbell

👁 Sights   🍴 Restaurants   🛏 Hotels   🛍 Shopping   🍸 Nightlife

★★★★☆   ★★★★★   ★★★★★   ★★★★★   ★★★★★

NEIGHBORHOOD SNAPSHOT

TOP EXPERIENCES

■ **Art and Murals in San Nicolas:** Take a self-guided (or guided) tour of San Nicolas to view the incredible outdoor art and murals that have rejuvenated the town.

■ **Try a Boozer Colada:** Stop by legendary Charlie's Bar to try this potent, signature cocktail and check out the cool collection of items left behind by customers over the past 70 years.

■ **Enjoy Seafood Straight from the Boat:** At Zeerovers in Savaneta you can watch fishermen bring in their catch and then pick exactly what you want for lunch.

■ **Relax at Baby Beach:** Rent some snorkel equipment to really experience all this beach's wonders.

■ **Shop for local Art and Crafts:** Visit Cosecha Creative Centre to view (and purchase) locally made arts and crafts; they even host workshops.

■ **Experience Mangel Halto's mangrove canals:** Kayak or paddleboard through the calm waters of Mangel Halto's mangrove canals; don't miss the secluded beach.

GETTING HERE AND AROUND

There is a public bus from downtown Oranjestad to Savaneta and San Nicolas, but it takes a long time. Taxis are pricey, but worth it if you're going for dinner and don't want to drink and drive. Another option is hiring a private driver for the day to explore the area.

If you do decide to drive, it should take about 15 minutes to get to Savaneta and about 20–25 minutes to get to San Nicolas from downtown Oranjestad.

QUICK BITES

■ **Mauchie Smoothies & Juice Bar.** This colorful roadside stand, just before the Savaneta turn, has excellent smoothies and fresh juices, as well as decadent shakes, burgers, and quesadillas. ⊠ *Savaneta 87, Savaneta*

■ **House of Cakes.** About 10 minutes past the airport en route to San Nicolas, this cheery little spot serves breakfast, baked goods, and authentic Aruban cakes by the slice. You can stay or take away. ⊠ *Rte. 1, Savaneta* ⊕ *houseofcakes. business.site*

■ **Saco di Felipe.** This hole-in-the-wall is *the* place for the best "sacos," paper bags full of fried chicken, ribs, chops, plantains, fries, and johnnycakes. It's the perfect snack before, or after, a night out. ⊠ *St Maarten Straat, San Nicolas* ⊕ *www.aruba. com/us/explore/ saco-di-felipe*

Savaneta, the island's original capital, is historically referred to as Commander's Bay since this is where the first Dutch Commanders resided. Farther south, the little ex-refinery town of San Nicolas is known locally as Sunrise City due to its brilliant sunrises. Today both towns are receiving renewed interest as tourist destinations as they begin to focus more on preserving and promoting the island's history, culture, and art.

Planning

Festivals and Street Parties

★ Aruba Art Fair

ARTS FESTIVALS | Organized by ArtIsa, this annual three-day event takes place each fall when artists from around the world are invited to collaborate on outdoor installations, sculptures, murals and more throughout San Nicolas. There are workshops with the artists, as well a Youth Art Fair that showcases the island's young aspiring artists. The event also includes an ArtFashion show that features the most creative works of local designers, and there are special events like pop-up restaurants and culinary art competitions. ⊠ *San Nicolas Promenade* ☎ *297/593–4475* ⊕ *www.arubaartfair.com.*

Island Festival

GATHERING PLACES | FAMILY | Get a mini taste of Aruba's carnival vibe on the last Wednesday of each month (7–10 pm) at this festival that showcases the parades and pageantry of the island's most beloved annual celebration as well as traditional and historical shows highlighting folk music and dance. There's local food, arts, crafts, and more, but all will take cash only. ■ **TIP➔ Many hotels offer return transportation packages.** ⊠ *Promenade San Nicolas, San Nicolas* ⊕ *www.islandfestivalaruba.com.*

★ Meet San Nicolas

GATHERING PLACES | As its name suggests this monthly festival, which takes place on the first Thursday of every month, is designed to introduce visitors to the town's local food, culture, art, and music. There is also special entertainment for kids. The event takes place in and around the public promenade in downtown San Nicolas. ■ **TIP→ No worries if you forgot to bring cash, there are several major bank ATMs in the downtown area near the promenade.** ⊠ *San Nicolas Promenade, Van de Veen Zeppenfeldstraat, San Nicolas.*

Carnival

GATHERING PLACES | Most of the main events during the annual Carnival take place in Oranjestad, but San Nicolas is considered to be the birthplace of the island's carnival traditions. Celebrations include a lighting parade, music competitions, and a mini-grande parade the day before the big one in Oranjestad. And, this the only location for Jouvert Morning, the annual sunrise road march that starts at 4 am—another reason the town was dubbed "Sunrise City." ⊠ *Savaneta.*

San Nicolas

During the oil refinery heyday, Aruba's oldest village was a bustling port and the island's economic hub. As demand for oil dwindled and tourism rose, attention shifted to Oranjestad and the island's best beaches. The past few years have seen a renaissance in San Nicolas largely due to the improvement of its infrastructure and the beautification of the main streets that have become an outdoor art district. There's also a new ballpark, the Museum of Industry, a brand-new cinema, and two new street festivals designed to introduce visitors to all the new charms of Sunrise City. A perennial draw has always been the legendary Charlie's Bar & Restaurant, a family-run business that's been around since 1941. The addition of Cosecha Creative Centre is also a draw for high-end, locally made art and crafts. The seafront area around Seroe Colorado is also earmarked for development in the near future.

Sights

★ Museum of Industry

MUSEUM | The old water tower in San Nicolas has been beautifully restored into a modern, interactive museum chronicling the different types of industries that have fueled the island's economy over

The beautiful murals found on San Nicolas's Art Walk began in 2015.

the past two centuries. Phosphate, gold, oil, and aloe all played major parts in the island's fortunes until tourism became Aruba's main economic driver. Displays include artifacts and profiles of colorful characters who played big roles in different eras; guided tours are offered (the last tour of the day starts at 5 pm). One of the highlights is the culture wall, a mural consisting of portraits of locals through the ages, all leading up the glassed-in walls of the old tower staircase. ⊠ *Water Tower, Bernhardstraat 164, San Nicolas* ☎ *297/584–7090* ☎ *$5* ◔ *Closed Sun.*

San Nicolas Art Walk

PUBLIC ART | In the past few years San Nicolas has seen an extraordinary revitalization and beautification thanks to new art initiatives organized by the local artist's foundation, ArtIsa. What began as a simple mural project in 2015 has since blossomed into the establishment of an annual Aruba Art Fair whose aim it is to create more public art projects. The incredible murals can cover entire buildings, and every year the collection grows. You'll find giant iguanas made from recycled materials, glowing lionfish, 3-D installations, interactive art, and many murals. It's an easy grid to walk on your own, or you can see where each installation is located on their online map. ∎TIP→ **You can see the installations on a leisurely walk, or on a guided walk with Aruba Mural Tours.** ⊠ *San Nicolas* ⊕ *arubaartfair.com/arubamurals.*

San Nicolas Community Museum

MUSEUM | This small community museum highlighting the town's past is located on the second level of the beautifully restored

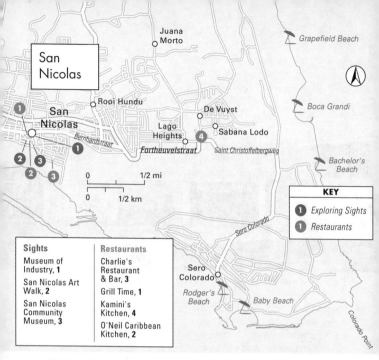

San Nicolas

San Nicolas

Juana Morto

Grapefield Beach

Rooi Hundu

De Vuyst

Boca Grandi

San Nicolas

Lago Heights

Sabana Lodo

Bachelor's Beach

Bernhardstraat

Fortheuvelstraat

Saint Christoffelbergweg

0		1/2 mi

0		1/2 km

Sero Colorado

KEY

❶	Exploring Sights
❶	Restaurants

Sero Colorado

Rodger's Beach

Baby Beach

Colorado Point

Sights	Restaurants
Museum of Industry, 1	Charlie's Restaurant & Bar, 3
San Nicolas Art Walk, 2	Grill Time, 1
San Nicolas Community Museum, 3	Kamini's Kitchen, 4
	O'Neil Caribbean Kitchen, 2

Nicolaas Store. Exhibit items include furniture, musical instruments, and personal items; worth checking out are the building's original flooring and wooden doors. The second floor terrace provides great views of the city. ■ TIP→ **The museum stays open later when there's a festival or special event happening.** ⊠ *B. van der Veen Zeppenfeldstraat 27, San Nicolas* ☎ *297/280–0018* 🖻 *$5* ⊙ *Closed Sun.*

🏖 Beaches

The beaches surrounding San Nicolas range from pristine soft sand edged by aqua waters to wild and windswept kitesurfing hot spots and romantic yet unswimmable picturesque escapes.

★ Baby Beach

BEACH—SIGHT | FAMILY | On the island's eastern tip (near the refinery), this semicircular beach borders a placid bay of turquoise water that's just about as shallow as a wading pool—perfect for families with little ones. A small coral reef basin at the sea's edge offers superb snorkeling, but do not pass the barrier as the current is extremely strong outside the rocks. The JADS dive shop offers snorkel and dive rentals; there is also a full-service bar and restaurant called the Lago Colony Beach Club and Rum Reef, a new adults-only infinity pool bar. You can also rent clamshell shade tents and lounges on the beach from Big Mamma Grill at the far end. **Amenities:** food and drink; showers; toilets; parking (free); **Best for:** snorkeling; swimming. ⊠ *Seroe Colorado*.

Bachelor's Beach

BEACH—SIGHT | This eastside beach is known for its white-powder sand. Snorkeling can be good, but bring a guide, and the conditions aren't the best for swimming as the currents can be strong. **Amenities:** none. **Best for:** snorkeling; windsurfing. ⊠ *East end, south of Boca Grandi*.

Boca Grandi

BEACH—SIGHT | This is *the* choice for the island's best kiteboarders and expert windsurfers, even more so than Fisherman's Huts. But the currents are seriously strong, so it's not safe for casual swimming. It's very picturesque, though, and a perfect spot for a picnic. It's a few minutes from San Nicolas proper; look for the big red anchor or the kites in the air. But be forewarned: the conditions are not for amateurs, and there are no lifeguards or facilities nearby should you get into trouble. **Amenities:** parking (free). **Best for:** solitude; walking; windsurfing. ⊠ *San Nicolas* ✛ *Near Seagrape Grove, on the east end*.

Grapefield Beach

BEACH—SIGHT | Just North of Boca Grandi on the eastern coast, a sweep of blinding-white sand in the shadow of cliffs and boulders is marked by an anchor-shape memorial dedicated to seamen. Pick sea grapes from January to June. Swim at your own risk; the waves here can be rough. This is not a popular tourist beach, so finding a quiet spot is almost guaranteed, but the downside of this is a complete lack of facilities or nearby refreshments. **Amenities:** none. **Best for:** solitude. ⊠ *Southwest of San Nicolas, on east end*.

Rodger's Beach

BEACH—SIGHT | FAMILY | Near Baby Beach on the island's eastern tip, this beautiful curving stretch of sand is only slightly marred by its proximity to the tanks and towers of the oil refinery at the bay's far side. Swimming conditions are excellent here. It's usually very quiet during the week, so you might have the beach all to yourself, but it's a local favorite on weekends. Full facilities can be found next door at JADS dive center strip on Baby Beach. **Amenities:** food and drink; toilets; parking (free). **Best for:** swimming; solitude. ⊠ *Seroe Colorado* ✛ *Next to Baby Beach*.

Baby Beach is a great spot for families.

🍽 Restaurants

During Aruba's oil boom, San Nicolas became a cultural melting pot as many workers brought their own flavors of food to the island. Today, you'll find everything from Jamaican and Trinidadian cuisines to South American and Asian, usually all with an Aruban twist. And, you'll find "sacos," a San Nicolas specialty that consists of a brown paper bag filled with finger-licking-good items like ribs, chicken, pork chops, johnnycakes, fried potatoes, corn on the cob, or plantains. Sacos are so well-known that locals and repeat visitors in-the-know often make a special trip from the other end of the island for them, usually with a stop at Saco di Felipe, a hole-in-the-wall spot that's been in business for six decades. Yes, its greasy, but that's the point, and it's addictive. Just don't ask for cutlery, as you're supposed to eat it all with your hands.

★ Charlie's Restaurant & Bar

$$$ | **CARIBBEAN** | Since 1941, Charlie's Bar has been the heart and soul of San Nicolas, famous for its interior decorated with the eclectic detritus left behind by years of visitors. But it also serves surprisingly good food, including superb fresh fish and shrimp, as well as killer steaks. **Known for:** a legendary San Nicolas institution; "Boozer Coladas," the signature drink; third-generation owner named Charles. $ *Average main: $25* ⊠ *Zeppenfeldstraat 56, San Nicolas* ☎ *297/584–5086* ☯ *Closed Sun.*

Grill Time

$$ | CARIBBEAN | As local a haunt as you can get, expect seriously authentic Aruban food including barbecue, *stobas* (stews), and *sopis* (soups), as well as a good selection of wraps, salads, and burgers. Order from the window and enjoy your feast at one of the outdoor picnic tables; wash it all down with an ice-cold local beer or one of the surprisingly creative cocktails. **Known for:** "saco"-style food (ribs, chicken, rice, beans, corn, johnnycakes, coleslaw) served in one container; local hangout where visitors are more than welcome; rotating daily specials. $ *Average main: $12* ⊠ *Bernhardstraat, San Nicolas* ✛ *Just before the main promenade downtown* ☎ *297/662–8626* ⊘ *Closed Mon.*

★ Kamini's Kitchen

$$ | CARIBBEAN | Housed in a cheery blue and green cottage, this charming spot is run by Kamini Kurvink who combines her Trinidadian heritage with local flavors to create unique Caribbean comfort food. Fish, seafood, and meat dishes are served with a spicy flair due to Kamini's secret signature hot sauces. **Known for:** hearty portions of homemade Caribbean specialties like goat curry and chicken roti; a great selection of vegetarian options; very warm, welcoming, and friendly staff and owner. $ *Average main: $12* ⊠ *De Vuyst 41B, San Nicolas* ☎ *297/587–1398* ⊘ *Closed Tues.*

O'Neil Caribbean Kitchen

$$ | CARIBBEAN | FAMILY | Right smack in the middle of the exciting new San Nicolas art walk, you'll find a warm and welcoming eatery, which is the ideal spot to get your Jamaican jerk on. You can also order real deal Jamaican dishes like ackee with salt fish and oxtail with beans, but the menu also has many local Aruban specialties like goat stew and fresh local fish and seafood. **Known for:** coconut-infused dishes like shrimp or chicken with rum and sweet chili sauce; real deal Jamaican specialties like ackee with salt fish; local favorite. $ *Average main: $15* ⊠ *Bernard van de Veen Zeppenfeldstraat 15, San Nicolas* ☎ *297/584–8700* ⊘ *Closed Mon.*

Hotels

Places to stay are few and far between in San Nicolas proper, but that might change in the next few years as there are big plans for an area that once housed Americans working at the oil refinery in Seroe Colorado in the '40s and '50s. With that said, if you really want to be in the area, you might find an Airbnb close to Baby Beach or Rodgers Beach. The closest boutique hotels are in Savaneta.

Seroe Colorado: A Ghost Town

This surreal ghost town was originally built as a community for American oil workers who came to run the Lago Refinery in the 1950s. There were 700 residents, an English-language school, a social club, a beach club, a hospital, a local newspaper, and a bowling alley. Today, organ-pipe cacti form the backdrop for the sedate white-washed cottages.

Many people visit to seek out the so-called **natural bridge.** (Another more famous bridge on the other end of the island collapsed into the sea a few years ago, but there are smaller, similar formations scattered around the island, including this one.) Keep bearing east past the community, continuing uphill until you run out of road. You can then hike down to the cathedral-like formation. It's not too strenuous, but take care as you descend. Be sure to follow the white arrows painted on the rocks, as there are no other directional signs. The raw elemental power of the sea, which created this fascinating rock formation, complete with hissing blowholes, is stunning. Many tours come out there to bring visitors to snorkel at Baby Beach in front of Seroe Colorado and there is a dive operator and restaurants on the beach there as well.

▶ Nightlife

Unless there's a street festival going on, San Nicolas's nightlife is confined to a few local spots that occasionally have live music outside like **Grill Time,** but the town is not really a place for bar-hopping as most of the little bars double as brothels that are part of the small but legal red-light district. However, when there is a scheduled street festival or annual event like the **Aruba Art Fair** or **Meet San Nicolas,** it's very safe for everyone including families after dark, and they are well worth attending. There is also a modern new cinema for first-run movies if you want to escape the heat for a while after a day touring or time at the beach.

● Performing Arts

Principal Cinema

FILM | After nearly three decades, locals are delighted to have a modern cinema in San Nicolas again. The air-conditioned cinema is state-of-the-art with large screens, VIP seats, and a modern concession stand. It's an ideal place to catch a flick before or after

Baby Beach. ✉ *Stuyvesant Straat 20, San Nicolas* ✛ *In the main promenade downtown* ☎ *297/523–6844* ⊕ *www.thecinema.aw.*

 ## Shopping

There are lots of mom-and-pop shops, clothing stores, small department stores, mini-markets and grocery outlets, modern pharmacies, and a few hardware stores scattered about, so you'll have no problem finding anything you forgot to bring out on a day trip. If you're seeking unique souvenirs, than San Nicolas is the place for locally made arts and crafts.

Artlsa

ART GALLERIES | Part art gallery, part administrative foundation, Artl-sa is responsible for the art and culture revolution in San Nicolas. The foundation displays local art for sale, hosts monthly exhibits for local artists, and is the spot to purchase tickets for the guided Aruba Mural Tours (also available online). ✉ *Bernard van de Veen Zeppenfeldstraat 14, San Nicolas* ✛ *Look for the stunning silver sculpture out front* ☎ *297/593–4475.*

★ Cosecha Store & Creative Centre

GIFTS/SOUVENIRS | Sister outfit of the downtown location, this arty emporium is a wonderful place to view and purchase made-in-Aruba art, crafts, jewelry, and more. Workshops for all ages are available on a regular basis so you can learn to work with different mediums and create your own unique Aruban souvenirs. ✉ *Bernard van de Veen Zeppenfeldstraat 20, San Nicolas* ✛ *Look for the giant pink flamingo head on the building* ☎ *297/587–8709* ⊕ *www. arubacosecha.com/cosechacreativecenter.*

Savaneta

It might be hard to believe that this sleepy little community on the southeastern coast was once Aruba's first capital city, but it was, until 1797. The Dutch commanders made their residences here and this is where the island's first stone house was built as the governor's residence. Today, this popular fishing spot is very much a local neighborhood with a laid-back, easy vibe and some new boho-chic places to stay. Cosmopolitan cafés are sidling up to heritage buildings, and new eco-activities and arty pastimes are also taking hold. There is talk of a new museum to trace the village's interesting past. Savaneta is also home to the island's only Olympic-size public swimming pool and the spot where they train their Olympic contenders—the island sent two swimmers to the summer Olympics in 2016. It's also home to the

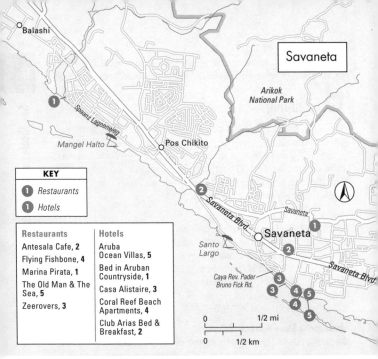

KEY
🔴 Restaurants
🔴 Hotels

Restaurants
Antesala Cafe, **2**
Flying Fishbone, **4**
Marina Pirata, **1**
The Old Man & The Sea, **5**
Zeerovers, **3**

Hotels
Aruba Ocean Villas, **5**
Bed in Aruban Countryside, **1**
Casa Alistaire, **3**
Coral Reef Beach Apartments, **4**
Club Arias Bed & Breakfast, **2**

Royal Netherlands Navy, the Netherlands Marine Corps, and the Netherlands Coastguard, so don't be surprised to see their ships gliding by often and close to shore, and don't be shy to wave… they like that.

🌞 Beaches

Savaneta is not really a beach community, as most of the swimming is done by jumping off a dock or deck, so don't except to see long strands of soft white sand like other parts of the island. Mangel Halto, and the little stretch at Santo Largo, are the exceptions.

Mangel Halto (*Savaneta Beach*)
BEACH—SIGHT | With a sunken wreck near the coast and a lot to see outside the bay, this is one of the most popular spots for shore diving, but be aware that currents are strong once you're outside the cove. It's also popular for picnics, and a wooden dock and stairs into the ocean make getting into the water easy. Sea kayak tours depart from here, and some outfits offer power snorkeling and regular snorkeling as well. There are stores within easy walking distance for food and drink. There are very few palapas, but you can take shade under the many trees and mangroves.

Amenities: none. **Best for:** snorkeling; swimming; water sports.
✉ *Savaneta* ✛ *Between Savaneta proper and Pos Chiquito.*

Santo Largo

BEACH—SIGHT | A small pristine beach in between Mangel Halto and Gouverner's Bay (just before Flying Fishbone) makes an ideal picnic spot far away from the crowds. Swimming conditions are good—thanks to shallow water edged by white-powder sand—but there are no facilities and virtually no shade. **Amenities:** none. **Best for:** swimming. ✉ *San Nicolas.*

🍴 Restaurants

Little cafés, snack bars, and Asian food take-outs can be found around the town, but for the best eats and fine dining head to the few waterfront spots peppered around the coastline.

★ Antesala Cafe

$ | INTERNATIONAL | FAMILY | The ideal spot to fuel up on gourmet coffee, fresh salads, wraps, and local delights on your way to Saveneta or San Nicolas. Don't let the modern-office-type building fool you: it's a restaurant that's air-conditioned and has free Wi-Fi. **Known for:** competent baristas serving sophisticated coffees; make-your-own pasta bowls; fresh and healthy fare. ⑤ *Average main: $10* ✉ *Savaneta 1-A, Savaneta* ✛ *On Rte. 1 east on the way to San Nicolas before Savaneta* ☎ *297/585–5909* ⊗ *Closed Sun.*

★ Flying Fishbone

$$$$ | INTERNATIONAL | Opened in 1977, this was the first restaurant in Aruba to offer feet-in-the-water dining, and that's why the legendary landmark is so worth the trek out to Savaneta for its insanely romantic seaside setting. An international menu is designed to please all palates, but the real culinary draw is fish straight from the island's most famous local fisherman's pier located a few doors over. **Known for:** "Savaneta's Seafood History" featuring the very local catch of the day; personal flambéed baked Alaska; tables set right in the ocean. ⑤ *Average main: $40* ✉ *Savaneta 344, Savaneta* ☎ *297/584–2506* ⊕ *www.flyingfishbone.com.*

Marina Pirata

$$ | CARIBBEAN | FAMILY | Locals and regular visitors in the know flock to this off-the-radar boathouse-style restaurant for fresh fish and seafood, as well as the melt-in-your-mouth fillet. Spectacular sunset views are a given, and kids love seeing the abundant fish swimming all around the pier and illuminated at night with underwater lights. **Known for:** fresh local lobster served different ways; great place for group celebrations; many squid dishes. ⑤ *Average*

Located in Savaneta, Mangel Halto is a popular spot for shore diving and picnics.

main: $23 ✉ Spanish Waters, Spaans Lagoenweg 4, Savaneta ☎ 297/585–7150 ⏱ Closed Tues.

★ The Old Man & The Sea

$$$$ | **CARIBBEAN** | This romantic toes-in-the-sand spot is also the main restaurant for Aruba Ocean Villas. Guests get first dibs at tables, but nonguests can make reservations (ideally far in advance), which is worth it to experience the incredible sea-food-centric cuisine that has made this place a legend. **Known for:** locally caught lobster; delicious Aruban fish soup; authentic keshi yena (cheese stuffed with spiced meat), the national dish. ⑤ *Average main: $65* ✉ *Savaneta 356A, Savaneta* ☎ *297/594–1808* ⊕ *www.arubaoceanvillas.com* ☞ *Reservations mandatory.*

Zeerovers

$ | **CARIBBEAN** | **FAMILY** | With a name that means "pirates" in Dutch, this small restaurant sits right on the Savaneta pier, where the local fishermen bring in their daily catch. The menu is basic: the day's fish and other seafood fried almost as soon as it's lifted out of the boat, with sides of local staples like plantains. **Known for:** freshest fish on the island; lively local hangout; picturesque sea view and sunsets. ⑤ *Average main: $10* ✉ *Savaneta Pier, Savaneta 270A, Savaneta* ☎ *297/584–8401* ⏱ *Closed Mon.* ▭ *No credit cards.*

Hotels

Most of the accommodations in the Savaneta area are private home rentals or rooms available via Airbnb, but there are a few notable exceptions.

★ Aruba Ocean Villas

$$ | RESORT | Secreted away in the sleepy little fishing village of Savaneta, Aruba's most unique new boutique luxury resort offers guests a surprising array of South Pacific–style accommodations including overwater bungalows, palapa-style beach villas, and even a tree house. **Pros:** insanely romantic setting, ideal for honeymoons; luxurious elite vibe yet friendly staff; far from the tourist fray. **Cons:** a car is needed; no pool in common area; no lunch available on-site. ⓢ *Rooms from: $350* ✉ *Savaneta 356A, Savaneta* ✛ *A few doors down from the Flying Fishbone restaurant* ☎ *297/594–1815* ⊕ *www.arubaoceanvillas.com* ⤴ *7 villas* ⦿ *Free Breakfast.*

Bed in Aruban Countryside

$ | RENTAL | In this charming complex, brightly colored cottage-style studios have their own kitchens, and guests have access to a garden patio and gazebos, a modern barbecue and large communal table—plus it's only a five-minute drive to Mangel Halto Beach. **Pros:** a great stay for animal lovers; authentic local experience; budget-friendly, clean, and well kept. **Cons:** not on a beach; you need a car to get around; no dining on-site. ⓢ *Rooms from: $70* ✉ *Seroe Alejandro 6, Savaneta* ☎ *297/593–2933* ⤴ *4 studios* ⦿ *No meals.*

★ Casa Alistaire

$$$$ | RENTAL | This incredible semi-overwater villa was once a private home and holds all kinds of surprises like a massive crystal chandelier hanging over a grand piano, a huge deck that fits about 20 people, a restaurant-size fully equipped kitchen, and four bedrooms, all decked out with their own theme. **Pros:** spacious retreat full of unique decor and luxury amenities; great swimming and snorkeling right off the deck; private chef catering and housekeeping available. **Cons:** you can smell the aroma of fried fish from Zeerovers; families with toddlers should be vigilant on the deck as it has no rails; far from shopping and nightlife (you need a car). ⓢ *Rooms from: $900* ✉ *Savaneta 258B, Savaneta* ☎ *297/594–1808* ⤴ *1 unit* ⦿ *No meals.*

Club Arias Bed & Breakfast

$ | B&B/INN | FAMILY | Though listed as a bed-and-breakfast, this modern little boutique resort in Savaneta's interior pleasantly surprises with amenities like a large pool, a wading pool, lush tropical landscaping, and spacious, tastefully appointed rooms and suites. **Pros:** breakfast included and served late or in bed; complimentary snacks and drinks by the pool; full concierge services. **Cons:** a car is a must; not on the beach; no hot water. ⑤ *Rooms from: $250* ✉ *123-K Saveneta, Savaneta* ☎ *297/705–5897* ⊕ *www.clubarias. com/index.html* ⤴ *10 rooms* ⦿ *Free Breakfast.*

Coral Reef Beach Apartments

$ | **HOTEL** | This beachfront complex with apartment-style rooms has a fully stocked communal kitchen for guests to self-cater and a tiny private beach and deck with an abundance of hammocks and picnic tables. **Pros:** bright, fresh rooms, some with great sea views; two large suites are great for families on a budget; maid service and Wi-Fi included. **Cons:** rooms do not have hot water; communal kitchen is not always convenient for everyone; not all rooms have sea views. ⑤ *Rooms from: $204* ✉ *Savaneta 344A, Savaneta* ☎ *297/584–7764* ⊕ *www.coralreefbeachapartments.com* ⤴ *8 units* ⦿ *No meals.*

Shopping

There's not much shopping per se around Savaneta save a handful of mini-markets and general supply stores. Occasional pop-up festivals with local farmers and craftspeople appear, but are not regularly scheduled.

Indira Skin Care & Art Gallery

SPA/BEAUTY | An enchanting surprise awaits on the road to San Nicolas just before the Savaneta turnoff in the form of this full-service spa and art gallery owned by the artist Merveline Geerman, who also happens to be a licensed skin-care specialist and masseuse. A full range of treatments are available including makeup and mani-pedis. ✉ *Savaneta 91, Savaneta* ☎ *297/584–6263.*

ARIKOK NATIONAL PARK AND ENVIRONS

Updated by
Sue Campbell

◉ Sights ⚑ Restaurants 🛏 Hotels 🛍 Shopping 🍸 Nightlife

★★★★★ ★☆☆☆☆ ☆☆☆☆☆ ☆☆☆☆☆ ☆☆☆☆☆

NEIGHBORHOOD SNAPSHOT

TOP EXPERIENCES

- **Go Wild:** Discover Arikok Park's untamed wilderness with a guided tour on foot or by vehicle.

- **Cool off in "Conchi":** Join a jeep safari trek to the surreal natural pool to swim or snorkel.

- **Hike the Haystack:** Climb Mt. Hooiberg—the second-highest peak on the island—for bragging rights and a great view.

- **Climb Casabari:** Discover odd rock formations that look like something out of *The Flintstones*.

- **Meet Cool Critters:** Visit the Donkey Sanctuary and the Ostrich Farm to make new animal friends.

- **Go Local:** Explore rural neighborhoods like Santa Cruz and Paradera to see how the locals live.

GETTING HERE AND AROUND

There are a few main highways that go through the island's deep interior, traveling through local neighborhoods, that lead to the national park entrance. Depending on where you are coming from—Palm Beach, Eagle Beach, or Oranjestad—it's best to check a map for the fastest route. It's also best to take a guided tour of the park first to get your bearings as it can be an unforgiving outback in many places, and definitely requires a four-wheel-drive vehicle. The Arubiana mapping app ⊕ *www.arubiana. com* is very helpful in this region and works offline as well.

QUICK BITES

- **Huchada Bakery.** Located about five minutes from Arikok National Park's entrance, this is the ideal spot for authentic Aruban baked goods and snacks. Ask a local for directions or use Google Maps to find it. ⊠ *Santa Cruz 328*

- **Urataka Center/ Best Pizza.** As the name suggests, this is a local favorite for pizza in Santa Cruz, but they also serve great snack platters and chicken. ⊠ *Urataka 12 A, Santa Cruz*

- **The Lionfish Snack.** "Eat 'em to beat 'em" is the motto behind this snack shack that serves only lionfish dishes to help combat the invasive species. It's only open Friday and Saturday so make sure to plan accordingly if you really want to eat here. ⊠ *Paradera 100, Paradera* ⊕ *www. thelionfishsnack- aruba.com*

First-time visitors are often surprised to discover how desertlike the other side of Aruba becomes once away from the landscaped grounds of the resorts with their swaying palms and brightly colored blooms. The island's interior and northeast coast are arid, rocky, and wild. But they have their own unique beauty, and are well worth exploring for surreal scenic vistas, romantic wave-whipped cliffs, and vast expanses of untouched wilderness.

Arikok National Park takes up approximately 20% of the island and is fiercely protected due to its fragile ecosystem; visitors must pay a park fee and abide by park rules in order to enjoy it. And although off-roading is allowed, first-time visitors should take a guided tour and learn the rules of the road, as driving on the dunes and on the beaches is highly discouraged. Within the park there are many surprises beyond cacti forests, dry riverbeds, and twisted divi-divi trees. There are cool caves like Fontein and Guadarikiri, a remote natural pool known as "Conchi," and Mt. Jamanota, the island's highest peak. Meandering goats and donkeys are common, but the park's elusive wildlife *is* easier to discover with the help of a guide. Park rangers offer free tours and man the entrances to the caves to enlighten about their ancient history.

Surrounding the park in the interior are neighborhoods worth exploring if you want to see how the locals live, like in Santa Cruz where you should sleuth out the numerous "snacks"—small food outlets that serve great homemade fare at very low prices. ■ TIP→ **Make sure you have cash. These spots don't take credit cards.** There's also Paradera, a small interior neighborhood where you'll find three natural attractions—the Casibari and Ayo rock formations and Mt. Hooiberg ("The Haystack")—all worth a visit on their own.

Arikok National Park

Aruba's national park encompasses 7,907 acres. Guests can explore the island's untamed wilderness by vehicle, horseback, or guided tour with a park ranger. The park's natural wonders include cool caves, a remote natural pool to swim and snorkel in, as well as the island's tallest peak, Mt. Jamanota, which is only recommended for experienced hikers.

There is only one restaurant within the park, and no lodging, so plan accordingly.

Sights

★ Arikok National Park

NATIONAL/STATE PARK | Covering almost 20% of the island's landmass, this protected preserve of arid, cacti-studded outback has interesting nature and wildlife if you know where to look. There are close to 30 miles of hiking trails within the park zone including a trek up Mt. Jamanota, the island's highest peak. Hiking maps for all levels of hikers are free at the visitor center, and in-depth maps of the park and its attractions are also available for download online at their website. It's highly recommended to take a guided tour on foot or by vehicle, as the roads can be very rough in some places; there are plenty of excursions by ATV, UTV, Jeep safaris, and more. A guided preview of what you can expect will help you if you want to return in your own rental car as well, but keep in mind that a 4x4 vehicle is a must and all visitors must pay a park entrance fee, which helps fund the park's eco-conservation. Some trails lead to glorious seaside coastal views, but a guided tour will help you understand the significance of the region and help you find attractions like the caves on the northeastern coast. There are no facilities past the visitor center, except one bar-restaurant at Boca Prins, so bring plenty of water and sunscreen and wear good shoes, as the terrain is very rocky. A new region near Spanish Lagoon has also been added recently as part of its protected area due to the importance of its freshwater canals and mangrove forests, but it is closer to Savaneta on the southwest coast, and not within the original park confines. ■**TIP→ You can book free guided hikes with a park ranger by phone or email, but must reserve 48 hours in advance.** ⊠ *San Fuego 70, Arikok National Park* ☎ *297/585–1234* ⊕ *www.arubanationalpark.org* 🎫 *$11* ⊗ *Park closes at 4 pm daily.*

Arikok Visitor Center

INFO CENTER | At the park's main entrance, Arikok Visitor Center houses offices, restrooms, and food facilities. All visitors must stop here upon entering so that officials can manage the traffic flow and hand out information on park rules and features. ☎ *297/585–1234* ⊕ *www.arubanationalpark.org* 🎫 *$10*.

★ Conchi (Natural Pool)

BODY OF WATER | The Natural Pool, also known as "conchi," meaning "bowl," was once a very secret spot due to its remote location, but today it's well visited by many ATV, UTV, and jeep safari tours. You can also reach it by horseback or on foot from the visitor center if you're up for a two-hour hike in the hot sun. (Best to get a park ranger to guide you there.) It's not really recommended to drive there on your own, even if you have a 4x4 rental, as the roads are rough and steep, but if you do, go early in the morning to avoid the touring crowd who typically start showing up around 10 am. Regardless of the crowd, it's worth the trip—the scene of wild surf crashing over ancient black volcanic rocks into a placid aqua pool is epic, and the spray of the cold sea water shooting over the top upon you when you're swimming or snorkeling is exhilarating. ■**TIP➜ Bring water shoes with a good grip; the rocks at the entrance to the pool are very slippery.** ⊠ *Arikok National Park, Arikok National Park* ☎ *297/585–1234* ⊕ *www.aruba.com*.

Fontein Cave

CAVE | FAMILY | This is the park's most popular cave as it's the only one with the drawings of Arawak Indians on its ceilings. The caves are accessible during park hours, and rangers are stationed outside the cave and can provide tours that explain the history of the cave drawings as well as discuss the resident stalagmites and stalactites. The cave floor is uneven, and there can be creepy crawlies underfoot, so closed-toe shoes are encouraged. ■**TIP➜ If you have time, check out the two-chambered Guadirikiri Cave; sunlight pouring through holes in the cave's roof lights the space.** ⊠ *Arikok National Park, Arikok National Park* ☎ *297/585–1234* ⊕ *www.arubanationalpark.org*.

Beaches

Boca Prins

BEACH—SIGHT | You'll need a four-wheel-drive vehicle to make the trek to this strip of coastline, which is famous for its backdrop of stunning sand dunes. Near the Fontein Cave and Blue Lagoon, the beach itself is small, but with two rocky cliffs and crashing waves, it's as romantic as Aruba gets. The water is rough, and swimming is prohibited. It's a perfect picnic stop, but it's also home to Boca

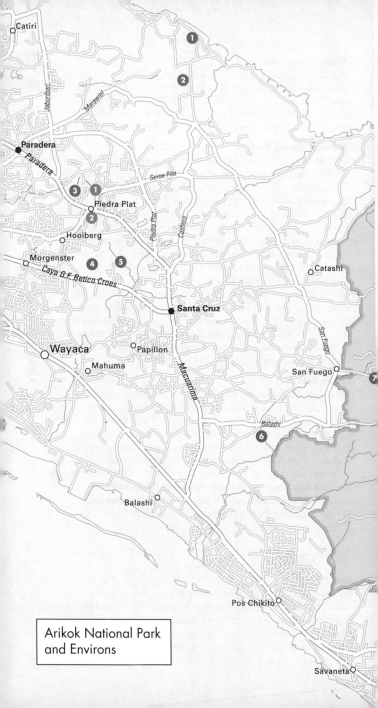

Arikok National Park
and Environs

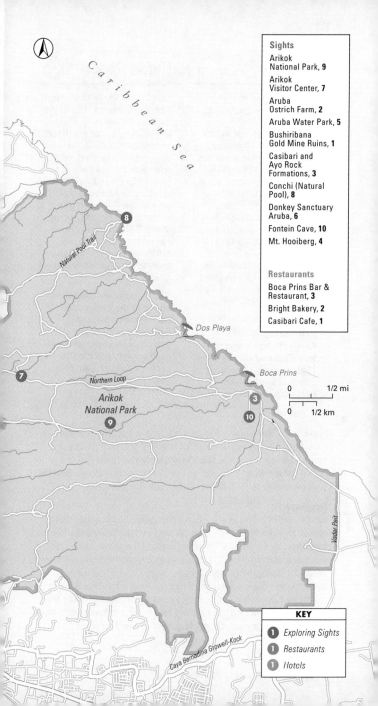

Caribbean Sea

Natural Pool Trail

Dos Playa

Boca Prins

Northern Loop

Arikok
National Park

Caya Bernadina Growell-Kock

Vader Piet

0   1/2 mi
0   1/2 km

Sights

Arikok
National Park, **9**

Arikok
Visitor Center, **7**

Aruba
Ostrich Farm, **2**

Aruba Water Park, **5**

Bushiribana
Gold Mine Ruins, **1**

Casibari and
Ayo Rock
Formations, **3**

Conchi (Natural
Pool), **8**

Donkey Sanctuary
Aruba, **6**

Fontein Cave, **10**

Mt. Hooiberg, **4**

Restaurants

Boca Prins Bar &
Restaurant, **3**

Bright Bakery, **2**

Casibari Cafe, **1**

KEY

1 *Exploring Sights*

1 *Restaurants*

1 *Hotels*

Exploring Arikok National Park

Visitors are free to hike on their own through Arikok National Park, and hiking maps are free at the Arikok Visitor Center. However, there's so much to see in the park in terms of flaora and fauna, and so many fascinating facts about the island's fragile eco-system and indigenous creatures, that a guide is invaluable. Luckily, free guided tours with a park ranger are available at the visitor center—reservations must be made 48 hours in advance—and are well worth it, especially for first-time visitors.

DID YOU KNOW?
Aruba is home to one of the world's rarest rattlesnakes. There are only about 200 Cascabel Rattlesnakes in existence, and they are only found naturally on this island. The park is home to the majority, but they are elusive and shy, and rarely stay out in the hot sun past 11 am. However, if you do hear a loud rattlesnake noise when you're passing a hole in the ground, don't freak out. Chances are good that it's a Aruban Burrowing Owl, or Shoco as it's known on the island. This quirky burrowing owl mimics the sound of a rattlesnake to keep predators away from its underground home.

The little red berries found on top of the Turk's Cap cactus are edible, and delicious. Just be careful if you try to pick them as these cacti are very prickly. The cacti are an important food source for the island's bird population.

Prins Bar & Restaurant, the only bar and restaurant in the entire park; you're bound to see a lot of the ATV and UTV excursions stopped there for lunch, too. Wear sturdy shoes, as the entrance is rocky. **Amenities:** food and drink; toilets; parking (free). **Best for:** walking; solitude. ✣ *Off Rte. 7A/B, near Fontein Cave.*

Dos Playa
BEACH—SIGHT | One of the most photogenic picnic spots on the island, this beach is two coves divided by limestone cliffs. One is treasured by surfers for its rolling waves; the other looks placid but has a current that is far too strong for swimming—you have to settle for sunbathing only. The best access is by four-wheel drive, as it's within the boundaries of rugged Arikok National Park. You might see locals surfing, but take care if you want to try as the current is very strong, and it's not for amateurs. **Amenities:** none. **Best for:** walking; solitude; surfing. ✣ *Just north of Boca Prins.*

The Natural Pool, or "conchi", was once a secret spot due to its remote location.

🍴 Restaurants

Though you can get some cold drinks and small snacks at the Arikok Park Visitor Center before you head out to explore the park, there is only one full-service restaurant (Boca Prins Bar & Restaurant) within in the entire park zone, and it's located on the far north coast.

★ Boca Prins Bar & Restaurant

$$$ | **INTERNATIONAL** | This inviting shaded oasis can appear like a mirage out of the arid outback, but you can believe your eyes, as it's really there, and it's the ONLY place in the entire national park for drinks and food, really good food! Burgers and big snack platters, authentic local specialties, cool signature cocktails, and cold local beer right beside Fontein Cave draw many of the ATV and UTV excursions to stop for lunch. **Known for:** Aruban specialties like keshi yena (stuffed Gouda cheese) and fresh fish; great views of the sea and surrounding desert; fun and friendly staff and full bar service; free Wi-Fi. $ *Average main: $23* ⊠ *Boca Prins, San Fuego 70, Arikok National Park* ☎ *297/593–2604* ⊕ *www.aruba. com.*

Arikok National Park's Dos Playa is a great spot for photos, picnics, and surfing.

Arikok National Park Environs: Santa Cruz and Paradera

The area surrounding Arikok National Park, including the towns of Santa Cruz and Paradera, offers offbeat attractions with unexpected animals and the island's second-highest peak, Mt. Hooiberg. There are also romantic secluded spots for picnics and unique scenic vistas for photo ops. ■ TIP→ **Make time to explore the local neighborhoods to see the cunucu (countryside) houses topped with terra-cotta-tiled roofs and often surrounded by fences made of cacti to keep the wild goats and donkeys out of the gardens.**

There are some places to grab lunch and snacks, but there aren't places to stay, shop, or go out at night, so plan to visit the area as a day trip.

Sights

Aruba Ostrich Farm

FARM/RANCH | FAMILY | Everything you ever wanted to know about the world's largest living birds can be found at this farm and ranch. There are emus, too. A large *palapa* (palm-thatched roof) houses a gift shop and restaurant that draws large bus tours, and tours of the farm are available every half hour starting at 9 am until 4 pm, seven days a week. Feeding the ostriches is fun, and you can also hold an egg in your hands. There is a full-service restaurant on-site. ⊠ *Matividiri 57, Paradera* ☎ *297/585–9630* ⊕ *www.aruba-ostrichfarm.com* 🎟 *$14.*

Aruba Water Park

AMUSEMENT PARK/WATER PARK | FAMILY | Completely refreshed and reopened in 2019 after years of closure, this big water park is themed around Aruba's gold rush days. It's a welcome respite from the heat in such an arid area, and an ideal spot to visit after hiking the "haystack" (Mt. Hooiberg). There are plenty of pools and waterfalls, as well as five slides, including the island's longest waterslide, food and drink spots, picnic areas, and a wooden playground. ■**TIP**➡ **The water park is part of Aruba Vacation Park, a Dutch vacation apartment village, but it's also open to the public.** ⊠ *Aruba Vacation Park, Santa Cruz* ✣ *At the foot of Mt. Hooiberg, near Aruba Vacation Park* ☎ *297/660–5570* ⊕ *www.arubavacation-park.com* 🕙 *Closed Mon. and Tues.*

Bushiribana Gold Mine Ruins

ARCHAEOLOGICAL SITE | You can view what is left of Aruba's onetime gold rush at the seaside ruins of a gold smelter; it's a great spot for photo ops. It's ironic that the Spanish left the island alone basically because they thought it was worthless; in fact, they dubbed it "isla inutil" (useless island) since they thought it had no gold or silver, but locals did find some long after the Spanish left. There is also a secret little natural pool nearby. ⊠ *North Coast, Bushiribana* ✣ *Near the California Lighthouse.*

Casibari and Ayo Rock Formations

ARCHAEOLOGICAL SITE | The odd-looking massive boulders at Ayo and Casibari are a mystery as they don't match the island's geological makeup in any other spot. They seem to have just cropped up out of nowhere, but they're cool to see and Casibari is fun to climb with man-made steps and handrails and tunnels set within the weird rock formation. Kids will love this all-natural jungle gym. You are not permitted to climb Ayo, but it's still worth a visit to see the ancient pictographs in a small cave (the entrance has iron bars to protect the drawings from vandalism). At the base of Casibari there's a café-bar-restaurant open for lunch and dinner, and the rocks around the outdoor dining area are lit up at night in neon colors. ⊠ *Paradera* ⊕ *www.aruba.com.*

★ Donkey Sanctuary Aruba

WILDLIFE-WATCHING | FAMILY | Take a free tour of the island's only donkey sanctuary where volunteers help abandoned and sometimes ill wild animals enjoy a happy forever home. This is a nonprofit organization and can always use help, whether financial or with chores. You can donate there or on their website, and you can even adopt a donkey—your donation goes to its annual feed

and care. Donkeys are fun, friendly animals and really enjoy visitors. It's a great family outing for all ages. ■TIP➜ **Bring carrots and apples for a really warm welcome from the residents.** ⊠ *Bringamosa, 2-Z Santa Cruz, Santa Cruz* ☎ *297/593–2933* ⊕ *main.arubandonkey.org/portal* ⧉ *Free.*

Mt. Hooiberg

NATURE SITE | Named for its shape (hooiberg means "haystack" in Dutch), this 541-foot peak lies inland just past the airport. If you have the energy, you can climb the some 562 steps to the top for an impressive view of Oranjestad (and Venezuela on clear days). It is the island's second-highest peak; Mt. Jamanota at 617 feet is the tallest. ■TIP➜ **It's a very hot climb with no shade, so wear a hat, apply plenty of sunscreen, and bring water.** ⊠ *Hooiberg 11, near Santa Cruz, Paradera.*

 Restaurants

The interior neighborhoods of Santa Cruz, before you enter the park, and Paradera nearby, are full of little snack bars, food trucks, cafés, small restaurants, and bakeries, so seek them out for an authentic local experience while you explore another side of Aruba.

★ Bright Bakery

$ | **CAFÉ** | This landmark family-run bakery has been a local favorite since it first opened in 1949, and it's still home to the island's most authentic baked goods including epic cakes, cupcakes, and pastries. There are also sandwiches and savory snacks like *pastechis* and hot dog *broodjes,* as well as fancy afternoon tea service, but reservations must be made 48 hours in advance for it. **Known for:** the largest collection of authentic Aruban cakes; wonderful homemade breads and buns; a cheery spot for breakfast. ⑤ *Average main: $10* ⊠ *Piedra Plat 44, Paradera* ☎ *297/585–9031* ⊕ *www.brightbakery.com.*

★ Casibari Cafe

$$ | **BARBECUE** | The bizarre rock formations at Casibari, which may make you feel as if you've dropped into Fred and Wilma Flintstone's dining room, make a great backdrop to this casual, offbeat restaurant, where wood-fired barbecue is king. Your generously portioned meal will be fire grilled under the stars, always accompanied by delicious sides that include coleslaw, Caribbean rice, and Casibari beans. **Known for:** offbeat alfresco atmosphere; hearty portions of grilled meats like barbecue ribs; authentic Aruban dishes like stew and keshi yena (they even have a vegetarian version). ⑤ *Average main: $15* ⊠ *Casabari Rocks, Paradera* ☎ *297/586–1775* ⊕ *www.casibaricafe.com* ⊙ *Closed Sun.*

Chapter 8

CASINOS

Updated by
Sue Campbell

Among the biggest draws in Aruba are the island's elaborate, pulsating casinos. Aruba offers up gambling venues closer in spirit and form to Las Vegas than any other island in the Caribbean. Perhaps it's the predominantly American crowd, but the casinos remain busy and popular, and almost every big resort has one. Although people don't dress up as elegantly as they did in years gone by, most of the casinos still expect a somewhat more put-together look (in the evening, at least) than a T-shirt and flip-flops.

Most casinos are found in hotels; all are along Palm Beach or Eagle Beach or in downtown Oranjestad. Although the minimum age to enter is 18, some venues are relaxed about this rule. By day "barefoot elegance" is the norm in all casinos, although many establishments have a shirt-and-shoes requirement. Evening dress is expected to be more polished, though still casual. In high season the casinos are open from just before noon to the wee hours; a few are open 24/7.

Aruba's casinos attract high rollers, low-stakes bettors, and non-gamblers alike, and the island is the birthplace of Caribbean stud poker. Games include slot machines and blackjack (both beloved by North Americans), baccarat (preferred by South Americans), craps, roulette—even betting on sports events. Restaurants and bars have added another dimension to the casinos; some of these venues offer live music, and most casinos serve free drinks while you play. Almost all casinos have a player's club where you can sign up for a free account (passport or driver's license required) for the ability to earn complimentary match-and-play coupons or free play on slots. Many casinos feature afternoon bingo with big prizes (these games draw many locals as well). Look in the local magazines and guides for coupons for free play or match-and-play offers. The majority of games and slots deal in U.S. dollars, but there are a few sections in some casinos where machines deal in florins, but the cashier will give you your winnings in U.S. dollars.

If you plan to play large sums of money, check in with the casino upon arrival so that you can be rewarded for your business. Some hotels offer gambling goodies—complimentary meals at local restaurants, chauffeured tours, and, in the cases of big spenders, high-roller suites. Even small-scale gamblers may be entitled to coupons for meals and discounted rooms.

The Good Bets

The first part of any viable casino strategy is to risk the most money on wagers that present the lowest edge for the house. Blackjack, craps, video poker, and baccarat are the most advantageous to the bettor in this regard. The two types of bets at baccarat have a house advantage of a little more than 1%. The basic line bets at craps, if backed up with full odds, can be as low as 0.5%. Blackjack and video poker, at times, have a house edge that's less than 1% (nearly a 50–50 proposition), and with bettor diligence can actually present a slight long-term advantage.

How can a casino possibly provide you with a potentially positive expectation at some of its games? First, because a vast number of gamblers make the bad bets (those with a house advantage of 5%–35%, such as roulette, keno, and slots) day in and day out. Second, because the casino knows that very few people are aware of the opportunities to beat the odds. Third, because it takes skill—requiring study and practice—to be in a position to exploit the opportunities the casino presents. Nevertheless, a mere hour or two spent learning strategies for the beatable games will put you light-years ahead of the vast majority of visitors who give the gambling industry an average 12% to 15% profit margin.

The Games

Baccarat

The most "glamorous" game in the casino, baccarat is a version of *chemin de fer,* which is popular in European gambling halls. It's a favorite with high rollers because thousands of dollars are often staked on one hand. The Italian word *baccara* means "zero." This refers to the point value of 10s and picture cards. The game is run by four pit personnel. Two dealers sit side by side at the middle of the table. They handle the winning and losing bets and keep track of each player's "commission" *(explained below).* The caller stands in the middle of the other side of the table and dictates the action. The "ladderman" supervises the game and acts as final judge if any disputes arise.

HOW TO PLAY

Baccarat is played with eight decks of cards dealt from a large "shoe" (or cardholder). Each player is offered a turn at handling the shoe and dealing the cards. Two two-card hands are dealt facedown: the "player" and the "bank" hands. The player who deals the cards is called the banker, although the house banks both hands. The players bet on which hand—player or banker— will come closest to adding up to 9 (a "natural"). Ace through 9 retain face value, and 10s and picture cards are worth zero. If you have a hand adding up to more than 10, the number 10 is subtracted from the total. For example, if one hand contains a 10 and a 4, the hand adds up to 4. If the other holds an ace and a 6, it adds up to 7. If a hand has a 7 and a 9, it adds up to 6.

Depending on the two hands, the caller either declares a winner and loser (if either hand actually adds up to 8 or 9) or calls for another card for the player hand (if it totals 1, 2, 3, 4, 5, or 10). The bank hand then either stands pat or draws a card, determined by a complex series of rules depending on what the player's total is and dictated by the caller. When one or the other hand is declared a winner, the dealers go into action to pay off the winning wagers, collect the losing wagers, and add up the commission (usually 5%) that the house collects on the bank hand. Both bets have a house advantage of slightly more than 1%.

The player-dealer (or banker) holds the shoe as long as the bank hand wins. When the player hand wins, the shoe moves counterclockwise around the table. Players can refuse the shoe and pass it to the next player. Because the caller dictates the action, player responsibilities are minimal. It's not necessary to know the card-drawing rules, even if you're the banker.

BACCARAT STRATEGY

To bet, you only have to place your money in the bank, player, or tie box on the layout, which appears directly in front of where you sit. If you're betting that the bank hand will win, you put your chips in the bank box; bets for the player hand go in the player box. (Only real suckers bet on the tie.) Most players bet on the bank hand when they deal, since they "represent" the bank and to do otherwise would seem as if they were betting "against" themselves. This isn't really true, but it seems that way. Playing baccarat is a simple matter of guessing whether the player or banker hand will come closest to 9 and deciding how much to bet on the outcome.

Blackjack

HOW TO PLAY

You play blackjack against a dealer, and whichever of you comes closest to a card total of 21 wins. Number cards are worth their face value, picture cards are worth 10, and aces are worth either 1 or 11. (Hands with aces are known as "soft" hands. Always count the ace first as an 11. If you also have a 10, your total is 21, not 11.) If the dealer has a 17 and you have a 16, you lose. If you have an 18 against a dealer's 17, you win (even money). If both you and the dealer have a 17, it's a tie (or "push") and no money changes hands. If you go over a total of 21 (or "bust"), you lose, even if the dealer also busts later in the hand. If your first two cards add up to 21 (a "natural"), you're paid 3 to 2. But if the dealer also has a natural, it's a push. A natural beats a total of 21 achieved with more than two cards.

You're dealt two cards, either facedown or faceup, depending on the custom of the casino. The dealer also gives herself two cards, one facedown and one faceup (except in double-exposure blackjack, where both the dealer's cards are visible). Depending on your first two cards and the dealer's up card, you can **stand,** or refuse to take another card. You can **hit,** or take as many cards as you need until you stand or bust. You can **double down,** or double your bet and take one card. You can **split** a like pair; if you're dealt two 8s, for example, you can double your bet and play the 8s as if they're two hands. You can **buy insurance** if the dealer is showing an ace. Here you're wagering half your initial bet that the dealer *does* have a natural. If so, you lose your initial bet but are paid 2 to 1 on the insurance (which means the whole thing is a push). You can **surrender** half your initial bet if you're holding a bad hand (known as a "stiff") such as a 15 or 16 against a high-up card such as a 9 or 10.

BLACKJACK STRATEGY

Many people devote a great deal of time to learning complicated statistical schemes. But if you don't have the time, energy, or inclination to get that seriously involved, the following basic strategies should allow you to play the game with a modicum of skill and a paucity of humiliation:

When your hand is a total of 12, 13, 14, 15, or 16, and the dealer shows a 2, 3, 4, 5, or 6, you should stand. *Exception:* If your hand totals 12, and the dealer shows a 2 or 3, you should hit.

When your hand totals 12, 13, 14, 15, or 16, and the dealer shows a 7, 8, 9, 10, or ace, always hit.

When you hold 17, 18, 19, or 20, always stand.

When you hold a 10 or 11 and the dealer shows a 2, 3, 4, 5, 6, 7, 8, or 9, always double down.

When you hold a pair of aces or a pair of 8s, always split.

Never buy insurance.

Craps

Craps is a fast-paced, action-packed dice game that can require up to four pit personnel to run. Two dealers handle the bets made on either side of the layout. A "stickman" wields the long wooden stick, curved at one end, which is used to move the dice around the table. The stickman also calls the number that's rolled and books the proposition bets made in the middle of the layout. The "boxman" sits between the two dealers, overseeing the game and settling any disputes.

HOW TO PLAY

Stand at the table wherever you can find an open space. You can start betting casino chips immediately, but you have to wait your turn to be the shooter. The dice are passed clockwise around the table (the stickman will give you the dice at the appropriate time). It's important, when you're the shooter, to roll the dice hard enough so they bounce off the end wall of the table. This shows that you're not trying to control the dice with a "soft roll."

CRAPS STRATEGY

Playing craps is fairly straightforward; it's the betting that's complicated. The basic concepts are as follows: If the first time the shooter rolls the dice he or she turns up a 7 or 11, that's called a "natural"—an automatic win. If a 2, 3, or 12 comes up on the first throw (called the "come-out roll"), that's termed "craps"—an automatic lose. Each of the numbers 4, 5, 6, 8, 9, or 10 on a first roll is known as a "point": the shooter keeps rolling the dice until the point comes up again. If a 7 turns up before the point does, that's another loser. When either the point or a losing 7 is rolled, this is known as a "decision," which happens on average every 3.3 rolls.

But "winning" and "losing" rolls of the dice are entirely relative in this game, because there are two ways you can bet at craps: "for" the shooter or "against" the shooter. Betting for means that the shooter will "make his point" (win). Betting against means that the shooter will "seven out" (lose). Either way, you're actually betting against the house, which books all wagers. If you're betting "for" on the come-out, you place your chips on the layout's "pass line." If a 7 or 11 is rolled, you win even money. If a 2, 3, or 12 (craps) is rolled, you lose your bet. If you're betting "against" on the come-out, you place your chips in the "don't pass bar." A 7 or 11 loses; a 2, 3, or 12 wins. A shooter can bet for or against himself, or against other players.

There are also roughly two dozen wagers you can make on any single specific roll of the dice. Craps strategy books can give you the details on come/don't come, odds, place, buy, big six, field, and proposition bets.

Roulette

Roulette is a casino game that uses a perfectly balanced wheel with 38 numbers (0, 00, and 1 through 36), a small white ball, a large layout with 11 different betting options, and special "wheel chips." The layout organizes 11 different bets into 6 "inside bets" (the single numbers, or those closest to the dealer) and 5 "outside bets" (the grouped bets, or those closest to the players).

The dealer spins the wheel clockwise and the ball counterclock-wise. When the ball slows, the dealer announces, "No more bets." The ball drops from the "back track" to the "bottom track," caroming off built-in brass barriers and bouncing in and out of the different cups in the wheel before settling into the cup of the winning number. Then the dealer places a marker on the number and scoops all the losing chips into her corner. Depending on how crowded the game is, the casino can count on roughly 50 spins of the wheel per hour.

HOW TO PLAY

To buy in, place your cash on the layout near the wheel. Inform the dealer of the denomination of the individual unit you intend to play. Know the table limits (displayed on a sign in the dealer area). Don't ask for a 25¢ denomination if the minimum is $1. The dealer gives you a stack of wheel chips of a color that's different from those of all the other players and places a chip marker atop one of your wheel chips on the rim of the wheel to identify its denomination. Note that you must cash in your wheel chips at the roulette table before you leave the game. Only the dealer can verify how much they're worth.

ROULETTE STRATEGY

With **inside bets,** you can lay any number of chips (depending on the table limits) on a single number, 1 through 36 or 0 or 00. If the number hits, your payoff is 35 to 1, for a return of $36. You could, conceivably, place a $1 chip on all 38 numbers, but the return of $36 would leave you $2 short, which divides out to 5.26%, the house advantage. If you place a chip on the line between two numbers and one of those numbers hits, you're paid 17 to 1 for a return of $18 (again, $2 short of the true odds). Betting on three numbers returns 11 to 1, four numbers returns 8 to 1, five numbers pays 6 to 1 (this is the worst bet at roulette, with a 7.89% disadvantage), and six numbers pays 5 to 1.

To place an **outside bet,** lay a chip on one of three "columns" at the lower end of the layout next to numbers 34, 35, and 36. This pays 2 to 1. A bet placed in the first 12, second 12, or third 12 boxes also pays 2 to 1. A bet on red or black, odd or even, and 1 through 18 or 19 through 36 pays off at even money, 1 to 1. If you think you can bet on red *and* black, or odd *and* even, in order to play roulette and drink for free all night, think again. The green 0 or 00, which fall outside these two basic categories, will come up on average once every 19 spins of the wheel.

Slot Machines

HOW TO PLAY

Playing slots is basically the same as it's always been. But the look and feel of the games has changed dramatically in the last several years. Machines that used to dispense a noisy waterfall of coins have given way to a new generation of machines that pay out wins with printed coded tickets instead of coins. In fact, machines no longer take coins on Aruba; a paper credit or paper money is all that is accepted unless you have credits on your player's card. Nowadays many of the games are all-digital and play like video games, with touch screens, and some have interactive features that even extend to the movement of your chair. Some can be so entertaining to play that you might forget that there is money involved, which, of course, is the point.

SLOT-MACHINE STRATEGY

The house advantage on slots varies from machine to machine, between 3% and 25%. Casinos that advertise a 97% payback are telling you that at least one of their slot machines has a house advantage of 3%. Which one? There's really no way of knowing. Generally, $1 machines pay back at a higher percentage than 25¢ or 5¢ machines. On the other hand, machines with smaller jackpots pay back more money more frequently, meaning that you'll be playing with more of your winnings.

One of the all-time great myths about slot machines is that they're "due" for a jackpot. Slots, like roulette, craps, keno, and

Big Six, are subject to the Law of Independent Trials, which means the odds are permanently and unalterably fixed. If the odds of lining up three sevens on a 25¢ slot machine have been set by the casino at 1 in 10,000, then those odds remain 1 in 10,000 whether the three 7s have been hit three times in a row or not hit for 90,000 plays. Don't waste a lot of time playing a machine that you suspect is "ready," and don't think if someone hits a jackpot on a particular machine only minutes after you've finished playing on it that it was "yours."

Video Poker

This section deals only with straight-draw video poker.

Like blackjack, video poker is a game of strategy and skill, and at select times on select machines the player actually holds the advantage, however slight, over the house. Unlike with slot machines, you can determine the exact edge of video-poker machines. Like slots, however, video-poker machines are often tied into a progressive meter; when the jackpot total reaches high enough, you can beat the casino at its own game. The variety of video-poker machines is growing steadily. All are played in similar fashion, but the strategies are different.

HOW TO PLAY

The schedule for the payback on winning hands is posted on the machine, usually above the screen. It lists the returns for a high pair (generally jacks or better), two pair, three of a kind, a flush, full house, straight flush, four of a kind, and royal flush, depending on the number of coins played—usually 1, 2, 3, 4, or 5. Look for machines that pay with a single coin played: one coin for "jacks or better" (meaning a pair of jacks, queens, kings, or aces; any other pair is a stiff), two coins for two pairs, three for three of a kind, six for a flush, nine for a full house, 50 for a straight flush, 100 for four of a kind, and 250 for a royal flush. This is known as a 9/6 machine—one that gives a nine-coin payback for a full house and a six-coin payback for a flush with one coin played. Other machines are known as 8/5 (eight for a full house, five for a flush), 7/5, and 6/5.

You want a 9/6 machine because it gives you the best odds: the return from a standard 9/6 straight-draw machine is 99.5%; you give up only half a percent to the house. An 8/5 machine returns 97.3%. On 6/5 machines, the figure drops to 95.1%, slightly less than roulette. Machines with varying paybacks are scattered throughout the casinos. In some you'll see an 8/5 machine right next to a 9/6, and someone will be blithely playing the 8/5 machine.

As with slot machines, it's optimal to play the maximum number of bets to qualify for the jackpot. You insert your ticket or bills and press the "deal" button. Five cards appear on the screen—say, 5, jack, queen, 5, 9. To hold the pair of 5s, you press the hold buttons under the first and fourth cards. The word "hold" appears underneath the two 5s. You then press the "draw" button (often the same button as "deal") and three new cards appear on the screen—say, 10, jack, 5. You have three 5s. With five coins bet, the machine will give you 15 credits. Now you can press the "max bet" button: five units will be removed from your credits, and five new cards will appear on the screen. You repeat the hold-and-draw process; if you hit a winning hand, the proper payback will be added to your credits.

VIDEO-POKER STRATEGY

Like blackjack, video poker has a basic strategy that's been formulated by the computer simulation of hundreds of millions of hands. The most effective way to learn it is with a video poker–computer program that deals the cards on your screen, then tutors you in how to play each hand properly. If you don't want to devote that much time to the study of video poker, memorizing these six rules will help you make the right decision for more than half the hands you'll be dealt:

If you're dealt a completely "stiff" hand (no like cards and no picture cards), draw five new cards.

If you're dealt a hand with no like cards but with one jack, queen, king, or ace, always hold on to the picture card; if you're dealt two different picture cards, hold both. But if you're dealt three different picture cards, hold only two (the two of the same suit, if that's an option).

If you're dealt a pair, hold it, no matter the face value.

Never hold a picture card with a pair of 2s through 10s.

Never draw two cards to try for a straight or a flush.

Never draw one card to try for an inside straight.

ACTIVITIES

On Aruba you can hike or bike a surreal arid outback and participate in every conceivable water sport, play tennis or golf, and horseback ride along the sea. But the big sport of note these days is beach tennis. Aruba has become the beach tennis capital of the Caribbean, and the island hosts several tournaments, including one big annual international competition. Snorkeling and diving are big of course, but there's also parasailing, banana boats, kayaking, paddleboarding, even yoga on paddleboard, touring submarines, luxury sails, golf, and even skydiving. And this island has some of the world's best conditions for windsurfing and kiteboarding, too. In fact, it has produced world champions. And the constant trade winds also make it an ideal destination to try the cool sport of *blokarting* (landsailing).

Biking and Motorcycling

Cycling is a great way to get around the island—though biking along busy roads is not encouraged. The new Linear Park paved trail from downtown Oranjestad all the way to the airport is ideal for families seeking a biking adventure along the sea. New Green Bike kiosks dot the island (there are eight stations now, with more to come), making it easy to grab a bike and deposit it at another station when you're done. If you'd rather cycle with less exertion, there are electric-bike rentals, too. Many resorts offer their guests coaster bikes for free (or for a low fee) to pedal around the beach

Relatively flat, Aruba can be the perfect biking destination.

areas, and there are also guided mountain bike tours that take you to the rugged interior. Or let your hair down completely and cruise around on a Harley-Davidson, either solo or with a group tour.

Rentals

There are plenty of dealers who will be happy to help you in your motoring pursuits.

George's Cycle Co

BICYCLING | This outfit has been renting motorcycles, scooters, and ATVs since the late 1980s. It's a reputable firm that offers great vehicles at good prices. Hotel pickup and drop-off is available. ⊠ *L. G. Smith Blvd. 124, Oranjestad* ☎ *297/593–2202* ⊕ *www.george-cycles.com* ✉ *From $55 per day.*

★ Green Bike Aruba

BICYCLING | It's no surprise that the first bike-sharing program in the Caribbean became popular very quickly, since Aruba is a Dutch-influenced island and people from the Netherlands adore their bikes. With more than 100 modern bikes at eight stations dotting the island (at busy tourist junctions including the cruise terminal), it's easy to swipe your credit card and hit the road. When you're done, park it somewhere else for the next person. Rentals are by the hour, but three-, five-, and seven-day passes and annual memberships are also available, as are guided bike tours. ☎ *297/594–6368* ⊕ *www.greenbikearuba.com* ✉ *From $24 (4 hours).*

Organized Excursions

Aruba Active Vacations Mountain Biking Tours

BICYCLING | FAMILY | Unless you are a skilled cyclist, it's best to join a tour to explore the island's arid, rugged, and unforgiving outback. This outfitter offers 2½-hour guided tours on top-quality Cannondale bikes with water and helmets supplied, including pickup and drop-off at your hotel. Points of interest include Alto Vista Chapel and the California Lighthouse, and the tour begins at the company's windsurfing shop at Fisherman's Huts. ⊠ *Fisherman's Huts Beach, Malmokweg* ☎ *297/586–0989* ⊕ *www.aruba-active-vacations.com* ⌂ *From $55.*

Bird-Watching

★ Birdwatching Aruba

BIRD WATCHING | The intimate outfit is run by Michiel Oversteegen, an award-winning professional wildlife photographer who can arrange private birding or nature photo tours with photo instruction as well. Tours are good for beginning birders as well as the most avid ornithologist, or anyone who wants to discover the island's surprisingly eclectic and abundant selection of birds. ■TIP→ **Pickup and drop-off included, but a max of five people allowed with a minimum of four hours; online booking only.** ☎ *297/699–2075* ⊕ *www.birdwatchingaruba.com.*

Bowling

★ Dream Bowl Aruba

BOWLING | FAMILY | Dream Bowl does it right with eight glow-in-the-dark bowling lanes, hip music, computerized scoring, and all kinds of special theme nights with prizes. It's part of the larger entertainment emporium on the top floors of the modern Palm Beach Plaza that includes a huge video arcade, a big modern sports bar, billiard tables, a food court, and prize machines. There is also a karaoke room and photo booth. ⊠ *Palm Beach Plaza, L. G. Smith Blvd. 95, Suite 310, Palm Beach* ☎ *297/586–0809* ⊕ *www.palmbeachplaza.com/listings/palm-beach-dream-bowl* ⌂ *From $35.*

Eagle Bowling Palace

BOWLING | FAMILY | Arubans love to bowl and often compete off-island. The Eagle emporium is the local favorite spot. Close to the high-rise strip, it has computerized lanes, a snack bar, and a cocktail lounge. Equipment rentals and group rates are available. ✉ *Sasakiweg, Pos Abao* ☎ *297/583–5038* 🖃 *From $35* ⌲ *Closed Mon.*

Day Sails

Aruba is not much of a sailing destination, though you will see a lot of luxury catamarans taking big groups of tourists out for a fun day of party sailing, snorkeling tours, or sunset dinner cruises. The main operators for large groups are DePalm, Red Sail, and Pelican. All have large catamarans, but some companies also offer old-fashioned wooden schooners for their day sails and snorkeling trips. There are a few smaller private yacht charters available as well. The weather is typically ideal, the waters are calm and clear, and the trade winds are gentle, so there's never really a bad time to hit the waves.

Many of these day sails include stops for snorkeling, but the companies recommended here offer more than just a snorkel tour, often including drinks, snacks, loud music, and sometimes dinner.

Day sails usually take off from either DePalm Pier, Hadicurari Pier, or Pelican Pier on Palm Beach. Many tour companies include pick-up and drop-off service at major resorts not on Palm Beach.

Chucky's Boat Rides
BOATING | Let Captain Hans personalize a private tour that can include snorkeling in off-the-radar spots and stops wherever you like for up to 10 people on his 25-foot deluxe boat called "Chucky." Private sunset tours and full day charters are also available. Departures are from Palm Beach. ✉ *Hadicurari Pier* ⚓ *Pier is beside MoomBa Beach Bar* ☎ *297/731–5000* ⊕ *www.chuckyaruba.com* ⌲ *From $200 for two.*

★ Full Throttle Tours
SNORKELING | Enjoy a different kind of thrill: a pontoon speedboat snorkel tour that blasts rock music while you bounce around the waves en route to numerous dive and snorkel spots around the island. A complimentary rum punch (in a souvenir cup) awaits you at the marina. Morning and afternoon trips available; tours take about three hours. Shorter sunset photo tours and private charters are also available. ✉ *Renaissance Marina, Oranjestad* ⚓ *Behind Lucy's Retired Surfer's Bar* ☎ *297/741–8570* ⊕ *www.fullthrottle-toursaruba.com* ⌲ *From $35 (sunset), $75 full tour.*

★ Jolly Pirates

SNORKELING | FAMILY | Aruba's unique, pirate-themed sailing adventure is a rollicking ride aboard a big, beautiful teak schooner complete with a wild and crazy swashbuckling crew and an open bar. The ships offer snorkeling tours with two or three stops and a rope-swing adventure, and the sunset cruises are also first-rate. Prepare to party hearty (it's basically impossible not to) due to their signature "pirate's poison" rum punch and infectious loud music. Snorkel trips always include the *Antilla* wreck. Departures are from Hadicurari Pier beside MooMba Beach Bar. ⊠ *Hadicurari Pier, Palm Beach* ⊹ *Office behind MooMba Beach Bar* ☎ *586–8107* ⊕ *www.jolly-pirates.com* ⊠ *From $32 (sunset sail) $45 (snorkel sail).*

Mi Dushi

SAILING | FAMILY | *Mi Dushi* means "my sweetheart" in the local lingo, and this operator has been offering guests snorkeling and sailing trips on Aruban waters for more than three decades. The company's vessel is a huge, colorful four-deck catamaran than can hold up to 70 people. Tours include music, an open bar, snorkel gear, instruction, and a pirate rope swing. Snorkel tours cover Aruba's three most popular reefs, and romantic sunset sails are also available. The morning tour includes a "Taste of Aruba" lunch. You can also charter them for private parties. Excursions depart from the Hadicurari Pier on Palm Beach. ⊠ *Hadicurari Pier, Palm Beach* ⊹ *Next to Marriott's Surf Club* ☎ *297/640–3000* ⊕ *www.midushi. com* ⊠ *From $41* ☞ *Children must be 4 years of age or older.*

Montforte III

SAILING | Take your sailing experience up a notch aboard this luxurious teak schooner that is designed to pamper. Exclusive tours take you to spots like Spanish Lagoon for snorkeling and kayaking, and around Boca Catalina for four-course dinners under the stars. Unlimited premium spirits, signature cocktails, tapas, and snacks are included in all trips, and there's sometimes live music onboard as well. Departure is from Pelican Pier. ⊠ *Pelican Pier, Palm Beach* ☎ *297/583–0400* ⊕ *www.monfortecruise.com* ⊠ *From $130.*

Sailaway Tours Aruba

SAILING | At 110 feet, the *Lady Black* is a beautifully retrofitted old-fashioned wooden schooner that's also the island's largest party ship. Enjoy an open bar and a big rope hammock on the bow while you sail with one of their snorkel, sunset, or dinner cruises. The friendly crew is happy to help you try some antics on the rope swing, and you can even hop on their backs while they do flips into the water. The party can get crazy. Available for private charters as well. ⊠ *Hadicurari Pier, Palm Beach* ⊹ *Look for their sign*

Snorkeling from a replica pirate ship will thrill any swashbuckler.

to check in across from MooMba Beach Bar in front of Hadicurari Pier ☎ *297/739–9000* ⊕ *www.sailawaytour.com* ✉ *From $64.*

★ Tranquilo Charters Aruba

SAILING | Captain Mike Hagedoorn, a legendary Aruban sailor, handed the helm over to his son Captain Anthony a few years ago after 20 years of running the family business. Today, *The Tranquilo*—a 43-foot sailing yacht—still takes small groups of passengers to a secluded spot at a Spanish lagoon named Mike's Reef, where not many other snorkel trips venture. The lunch cruise to the south side always includes "Mom's famous Dutch pea soup," and they also do private charters for dinner sails and sailing trips around Aruba's lesser-explored coasts. Look for the red boat docked at the Renaissance Marina beside the Atlantis Submarine launch. ✉ *Renaissance Marina, Oranjestad* ☎ *297/586–1418* ⊕ *www.tranquiloaruba.com* ✉ *From $85.*

Fishing

Deep-sea catches here include anything from barracuda, tuna, and wahoo to kingfish, sailfish, and marlins. A few skippered charter boats are available for half- or full-day excursions. Package prices vary but typically include tackle, bait, and refreshments.

★ Driftwood Charters

FISHING | Driftwood is a tournament-rigged, 35-foot yacht manned by Captain Herby, who is famous for offering deep-sea fishing charters on Aruba since the early 1990s. He is also co-owner of Driftwood Restaurant and is always happy to bring your catch to their chef for expert preparation so you can enjoy it for dinner the very same night. Charters can accommodate up to six people. ⊠ *Seaport Marina, Oranjestad* ☎ *297/583–2515* ⊕ *www.driftwoodfishingcharters.com/* ☒ *From $400.*

Teaser Fishing Charters Aruba

FISHING | FAMILY | The expertise of the Teaser crew is matched by a commitment to sensible fishing practices, which include catch and release and avoiding ecologically sensitive areas. The company's yacht is fully equipped, and the crew seem to have an uncanny ability to locate the best fishing spots with Captain Milton at the helm. ⊠ *Renaissance Marina, Oranjestad* ☎ *297/593–9228* ⊕ *www.teaserfishingaruba.com* ☒ *From $400 (limit 6 people).*

Golf

Golf may seem incongruous on an arid island such as Aruba, yet there are two popular courses.

The Links at Divi Aruba

GOLF | This 9-hole course was designed by Karl Litten and Lorie Viola. The par-36 flat layout stretches to 2,952 yards and features paspalum grass (best for seaside courses) and takes you past beautiful lagoons. It's a testy little course with water abounding, making accuracy more important than distance. Amenities include a golf school with professional instruction, a driving range, a practice green, and a two-story golf clubhouse with a pro shop. Two restaurants are available: Windows on Aruba for fine dining and Mulligan's for a casual and quick lunch. ⊠ *Divi Village Golf & Beach Resort, J. E. Irausquin Blvd. 93, Druif* ☎ *297/581–4653* ⊕ *www.divilinks.com* ☒ *From $80 low season* ⛳ *9 holes, 2952 yards, par 36.*

★ Tierra del Sol

GOLF | Stretching out to 6,811 yards, this stunning course is situated on the northwest coast near the California Lighthouse and is Aruba's only 18-hole course. Designed by Robert Trent Jones Jr., Tierra del Sol combines Aruba's native beauty (cacti and rock formations, stunning views) with good greens and beautiful landscaping. Wind can also be a factor here on the rolling terrain, as are the abundant bunkers and water hazards. Greens fees include a golf cart equipped with GPS and a communications system that allows you to order drinks for your return to the clubhouse. The fully stocked golf shop is one of the Caribbean's most elegant, with an extremely attentive staff. This course hosts numerous events including the annual Aruba International Pro-Am Golf Tournament every August. ⊠ *Tierra del Sol Resort, Caya di Solo 10, Malmok-weg* ☎ *297/586–7800* ⊕ *www.tierradelsol.com/golf* ☑ *From $79 for 9 holes* ⅃ *18 holes, 6811 yards, par 71.*

Hiking

Despite Aruba's arid landscape, hiking the rugged countryside will give you the best opportunities to see the island's wildlife and flora. Arikok National Park is an excellent place to glimpse the real Aruba, free of the trappings of tourism. The heat can be oppressive, so be sure to take it easy, wear a hat, and have a bottle of water handy. Get maps and information at Arikok National Park Visitor Center. ■ TIP→ **Guided hikes are recommended for those with little hiking experience.** Beyond Arikok National Park, the 500-step trek up Mt. Hooiberg (locals call it "The Haystack") is also a good workout that rewards with fabulous island views.

★ Arikok National Park

HIKING/WALKING | FAMILY | There are more than 20 miles of trails concentrated in the island's eastern interior and along its northeastern coast. Arikok Park is crowned by Aruba's second-highest mountain, the 577-foot Mt. Arikok, so you can also go climbing there. Hiking in the park, whether alone or in a group led by guides, is generally not too strenuous, but it is hot. You'll need sturdy shoes to grip the granular surfaces and climb the occasionally steep terrain. You should also exercise caution with the strong sun—bring along plenty of water and wear sunscreen and a hat. At the park's main entrance, the Arikok Visitor Center houses exhibits, restrooms, and food concessions, and provides maps and marked trail information, park rules, and features. Free guided minitours are the best way to get oriented at the park entrance. Tour operators also offer four-wheeling and horseback tours across the rugged Arikok landscape. You can also download hiking maps from their website for self-guided tours. ⊠ *Santa Cruz* ☎ *297/585–1234* ⊕ *www.arubanationalpark.org* ☑ *$11 park entrance, $28 year pass* ⊙ *Park closes at 4 pm.*

Horseback Riding

Ranches offer short jaunts along the beach or longer rides through the countryside and even to the ruins of an old gold mill. Riders of all experience levels will be thrilled that most of Aruba's horses are descendants of the Spanish Paso Fino—meaning "fine step"—which offer a supersmooth ride even at a trot!

Rancho Daimari

HORSEBACK RIDING | FAMILY | This operation offers some unique horseback riding tours on Aruba. Choose from a trek to the incredible natural pool in the heart of Arikok National Park, or to a scenic and secret surfer's beach. Tours are very family-friendly and accommodate all levels of riding skills. Complimentary return transportation from hotels. Reservations mandatory; maximum eight people per tour. ⊠ *Paseo Herencia (office), J. E. Irausquin Blvd. 382-A* ☎ *297/586–6284* ⊕ *www.ranchodaimariaruba.com* 🖾 *From $105.*

★ Rancho La Ponderosa

HORSEBACK RIDING | FAMILY | Run by one of Aruba's best-known horsemen—and using steeds from his private stock—Rancho La Ponderosa offers quality rides of two or two-and-a-half hours. Choose from a route along the wild coast to gold mill ruins and a fallen land bridge, or ride to the famous ostrich farm. It's noteworthy that these tours never encounter vehicular traffic. ⊠ *Papaya 30, Paradera* ☎ *297/587–1142* ⊕ *www.rancholaponderosa.com* 🖾 *From $80.*

Rancho Loco

HORSEBACK RIDING | FAMILY | Surrounded by a lush fruit and vegetable farm, Rancho Loco is touted as the "greenest ranch in Aruba." This equestrian center also gives lessons and boards and trains horses. Their tours range from sunset jaunts on Moro Beach to Arikok Park interior treks including trips to the Natural Pool. Private rides also available. ⊠ *Sombre 22-e, Santa Cruz* ☎ *297/592–6039* ⊕ *www.rancholocoaruba.com/en* ⌨ *From $75.*

Kayaking

Kayaking is a popular sport on Aruba, especially because the waters are so calm. It's a great way to explore the coast and the mangroves.

Aruba Outdoor Adventures

KAYAKING | FAMILY | This small, family-run outfitter offers a unique combination of small-group (six people max) pedal-kayaking and snorkel tours along the island's southeastern coast. Mangroves and reef explorations take you around calm water near Mangel Halto, Savaneta, and Barcadera; well-informed guides explain the natural environment and help guests navigate the snorkeling

The calm waters and mangrove lagoons found along Aruba's southern coast are perfect for kayaking.

portions. No kayaking experience is necessary. Pickup and drop-off are included, as well as snorkel equipment, a dry bag, snacks, and drinks. Departures are from the DePalm Island Ferry Terminal outside Oranjestad. ⊠ *DePalm Island Ferry Terminal, Balashi* ☎ *297/749–6646* ⊕ *www.arubaoutdooradventures.com* ✉ *From $100.*

★ Clear Kayak Aruba

KAYAKING | FAMILY | This is the only Aruba outfitter that offers clear-bottom sea kayaks, and the only one offering night tours as well. By day, groups paddle through the natural mangroves at Mangel Halto with a guide who can tell you how the roots create a natural nursery for juvenile marine life; the route also passes over lots of big, healthy coral full of colorful tropical fish. A second tour begins at Arashi Beach at dusk; then, after dark, the kayaks are lit up with LED lights that attract marine life to their clear bottoms. You must be age 12 or older to participate. ⊠ *Savaneta 402, Savaneta* ☎ *297/566–2205* ⊕ *www.clearkayakaruba.com* ✉ *From $60.*

Multisport Outfitters

There are a number of outfitters in Aruba that can handle nearly all your water- or land-based activities with guided excursions and rental equipment. Here is a list of a few of our favorites.

★ De Palm Tours

BOATING | FAMILY | Aruba's premier tour company covers every inch of the island on land and under sea, and they even have their own submarine (Atlantis) and semi-submarine (*Seaworld Explorer*) and their own all-inclusive private island destination (De Palm Island), which has great snorkeling as well as Seatrek, a cool underwater air-supplied-helmet walk. Land exploration options include air-conditioned bus sightseeing tours and rough and rugged outback jaunts by jeep safari to popular attractions like the natural pool. You can also do off-road tours in a UTV (two-seater utility task vehicle) via their guided caravan trips. On the waves, their luxury catamaran *De Palm Pleasure* offers romantic sunset sails and snorkel trips that include an option to try SNUBA—deeper snorkeling with an air-supplied raft at Aruba's most famous shipwreck. De Palm also offers airport transfers and private VIP transfers. ⊠ *L. G. Smith Blvd. 142, Oranjestad* ☎ *297/582–4400* ⊕ *www. depalmtours.com.*

EL Tours

PARK—SPORTS-OUTDOORS | This tour and transfer company offers a wide range of tours to explore Aruba including hiking, UTV tours, beach-hopping jaunts, jeep safaris, and island highlights. Personalized custom tours and VIP airport transfers are also available. ⊠ *Barcadera 4, Oranjestad* ☎ *297/585–6731* ⊕ *www.eltoursaruba. com.*

Pelican Adventures

SCUBA DIVING | FAMILY | In operation since 1984, this company arranges sailing and boating charters for fishing and exploring, as well as jeep adventures and guided excursions to Aruba's caves and historic sites. Scuba and snorkeling trips are available for divers of all levels. Novices start with midmorning classes and then move to the pool to practice what they've learned; by afternoon they put their new skills to use at a shipwreck off the coast. The company is also known for its fun Havana-style sunset cruises and also a dinner cruise that chases the sunset then ends with a meal at the company's pier restaurant, Pelican Nest Seafood Grill. ⊠ *Pelican Pier, Palm Beach* ✚ *Near the Holiday Inn and Playa Linda hotels* ☎ *297/586–3271* ⊕ *www.pelican-aruba. com* 🖃 *From $50.*

★ Red Sail Sports Aruba

BOATING | A dynamic company established in 1989, they are experts in the field of water-sports recreation. They offer excellent diving excursions, snorkel sails, sunset sails, and full dinner sails, and they are the premier spot for Jetlev-jet packs (over the water), jet blades, and hoverboards with instruction (weekdays).

Aruba is known as one of the Caribbean's wreck diving capitals.

The company also has its own sports-equipment shops. ✉ *J. E. Irausquin Blvd. 348-A, Palm Beach* ☎ *297/586–1603* ⊕ *www. redsailaruba.com.*

Scuba Diving and Snorkeling

With visibility of up to 90 feet, the waters around Aruba are excellent for snorkeling and diving. In fact, Aruba is known as one of the wreck diving capitals of the Caribbean. Advanced and novice divers alike will find plenty to occupy their time, as many of the most popular sites—including some interesting shipwrecks—are found in shallow waters ranging from 30 to 60 feet. Coral reefs covered with sensuously waving sea fans and eerie giant sponge tubes attract a colorful menagerie of sea life, including gliding manta rays, curious sea turtles, shy octopuses, and fish from grunts to groupers. Marine preservation is a priority on Aruba, and regulations by the Conference on International Trade in Endangered Species make it unlawful to remove coral, conch, and other marine life from the water.

Day sail operators often offer snorkeling, and it's usually coupled with an open bar and loud music; almost all of them stop at the famous *Antilla* shipwreck just offshore, which provides a rare treat for snorkelers to be able to view a wreck typically only divers would be able to access. Some dive operators also allow snorkelers to tag along with divers on a trip for a lower fee as well.

Major West-Side Dive Sites

Airplane Wrecks. Two planes purposely scuttled to create a new dive site are still somewhat intact around Renaissance Private Island. You must do a drift dive to see them; they broke apart somewhat after Hurricane Lenny caused big swells in the area.

***Antilla* Wreck.** This German freighter, which sank off the northwest coast near Malmok Beach, is popular with both divers and snorkelers. Some outfits also offer SNUBA, which allows you to get a bit closer to the wreck if you are not certified to dive. When Germany declared war on the Netherlands in 1940 during World War II it was stationed off the coast where it still is now. The captain chose to sink the ship on purpose before Aruban officials could board and seize it. The 400-foot-long vessel—referred to by locals as "the ghost ship"—broke into two distinct halves. It has large compartments, and you can climb into the captain's bathtub, which sits beside the wreck, for a unique photo op. Lobster, angelfish, yellowtail, and other fish swim about the wreck, which is blanketed by giant tube sponges and coral.

Black Beach. The clear waters just off this beach are dotted with sea fans. The area takes its name from the rounded black stones lining the shore. It's the only bay on the island's north coast sheltered from thunderous waves, making it a safe spot for diving.

***Californian* Wreck.** Although this steamer is submerged at a depth that's perfect for underwater photography, this site is safe only for advanced divers; the currents here are strong, and the waters are dangerously choppy. This wreck is what the famous lighthouse is named for.

Malmok Reef (*Debbie II* Wreck). Lobsters and stingrays are among the highlights at this bottom reef adorned by giant green, orange, and purple barrel sponges as well as leaf and brain coral. From here you can spot the *Debbie II,* a 120-foot barge that sank in 1992.

***Pedernales* Wreck.** During World War II, this oil tanker was torpedoed by a German submarine. The U.S. military cut out the damaged centerpiece, towed the two remaining pieces to the States, and welded them together into a smaller vessel that eventually transported troops during the invasion of Normandy. The section that was left behind in shallow water is now surrounded by coral formations, making this a good site for novice divers. The ship's cabins, washbasins, and pipelines are exposed. The area teems with grouper and angelfish. It's also a good site for snorkelers since it's easily visible from the shallows.

Tugboat Wreck. Spotted eagle rays and stingrays are sometimes observed at this shipwreck at the foot of Harbour Reef, which is one of Aruba's most popular. Spectacular formations of brain, sheet, and star coral blanket the path to the wreck, which is inhabited by several bright-green moray eels.

East-Side Dive Sites

Jane C. **Wreck.** This 200-foot freighter, lodged in an almost vertical position at a depth of 90 feet, is near the coral reef west of De Palm Island. Night diving is exciting here, as the polyps emerge from the corals that grow profusely on the steel plates of the decks and cabins. Soft corals and sea fans are also abundant in the area. The current is strong, and this is for advanced divers only.

Punta Basora. This narrow reef stretches far into the sea off the island's easternmost point. On calm days you'll see eagle rays, stingrays, barracudas, and hammerhead sharks, as well as hawks-bill and loggerhead turtles.

The Wall. From May to August, green sea turtles intent on laying their eggs abound at this steep-walled reef. You'll also spot groupers and burrfish swimming nearby. Close to shore, massive sheet corals are plentiful; in the upper part of the reef are colorful varieties such as black coral, star coral, and flower coral. Flitting about are brilliant damselfish, rock beauties, and porgies.

Recommended Dive Operators

★ Aruba Watersports Center
BICYCLING | FAMILY | This family-run, full-service water sports outfitter is right on Palm Beach, offering a comprehensive variety of adventures including small group PADI dives and snorkeling trips, but also WaveRunners, tubing, Hobie Cat sailing, stand-up paddleboarding, kayaking, wakeboarding, and parasailing. Snorkeling trips aboard the *Arusun* are for small groups, and the boat goes to spots others don't, including the *Pederanles* wreck. ⊠ *L. G. Smith Blvd. 81B, Palm Beach* ⚓ *Between Barcelo and Hilton resorts* ☎ *297/586–6613* ⊕ *www.arubawatersportscenter.com* ⊠ *From $20.*

Dive Aruba
SCUBA DIVING | Resort courses, certification courses, and trips to interesting shipwrecks make Dive Aruba worth checking out. The outfitter only offers small group dives. They target a different dive

site every day of the week (except Sunday). Free hotel pickup and drop-off available. ✉ *Wilhelminastraat 8, Oranjestad* ☎ *297/582–7337* ⊕ *www.divearuba.com.*

★ JADS Dive Center

SCUBA DIVING | Owned by the local Fang family, JADS has been in operation for decades and is famous for its intro to dive package that takes you to one of the island's only shore diving sites at Mangel Halto, which has easy access for beginners. JADS also offers all levels of PADI dive instruction, a children's program, and personalized boat dive trips and guided night dives. Located right on Baby Beach, there's a full-service dive shop with snorkel equipment rentals. Rum Reef, an infinity pool bar, is next door. ■TIP→ **Looking for a unique souvenir? One dive instructor sells handmade jewelry made from lionfish skin in the dive shop; the craft helps rid the environment of these destructive fish.** ✉ *Seroe Colorado 245E, Seroe Colorado* ☎ *297/584–6070* ⊕ *www.jadsaruba.com* ☞ *From $59.*

Native Divers Aruba

SCUBA DIVING | A small, personal operation, Native Divers Aruba specializes in PADI open-water courses. Ten different certification options include specialties like Multilevel Diver, Search & Recovery Diver, and Underwater Naturalist. Their boat schedule is also flexible, and it's easy to tailor instruction to your specific needs. They also allow snorkelers to tag along and provide all the necessary equipment. ✉ *Marriott Surf Club, Palm Beach* ✛ *On the beach in front of Marriott Surf Club* ☎ *297/586–4763* ⊕ *www.nativedivers.com* ☞ *From $80.*

S.E. Aruba Fly 'n Dive

SCUBA DIVING | One of the island's oldest diving operators, S.E. Aruba Fly 'n Dive offers a full range of PADI courses as well as many specialty courses like Nitrox Diver, Wreck Diver, and Deep Diver. Private snorkeling trips are available, and they can also instruct you in rescue techniques, becoming an underwater naturalist, or underwater photography. ✉ *L. G. Smith Blvd. 1A, Oranjestad* ☎ *297/588–1150* ⊕ *www.se-aruba.com* ☞ *From $90.*

Skydiving

★ SkyDive Aruba

FLYING/SKYDIVING/SOARING | There's nothing like the adrenaline rush when you are forced to jump out of a perfectly good airplane at 10,000 feet because you are attached to your instructor. You have no choice but to free-fall at 120 mph toward the island for 35 seconds until your chute opens, and then your downward journey has you floating to the sand in a little over five minutes. Afterward you can purchase a video of your courageous leap. Group discounts are available. Hotel pickup and drop-off are included. ✉ *Malmok Beach, Malmokweg* ☎ *297/735–0654* ⊕ *www.skydivearuba.com* 🎬 *From $299*.

Submarine Excursions

★ Atlantis Submarines

TOUR—SPORTS | Enjoy the deep without getting wet in a real U.S. Coast Guard–approved submarine with *Atlantis*, run by De Palm Tours and operating on the island for over 25 years. The underwater reefs are teeming with marine life, and the 65-foot air-conditioned sub takes up to 48 passengers for a voyage 130 feet into the deep to view shipwrecks and amazing sights with informative narration. The company also owns the *Seaworld Explorer*, a semi-submersible that allows you to sit and view Aruba's marine habitat from 5 feet below the surface. (Children must be a minimum of 36 inches tall and four years old.) ✉ *Renaissance Marina, L. G. Smith Blvd. 82, Oranjestad* ☎ *297/583–6090* ⊕ *www.depalmtours. com/pages/atlantis-submarines-expedition* 🎬 *From $105*.

Tennis

★ Aruba Racquet Club

TENNIS | Aruba's winds make tennis a challenge even if you have the best of backhands. Although visitors can make arrangements to play at the resorts, priority goes to guests. Some private tennis clubs can also accommodate you, or you can try the facilities at the Aruba Racquet Club. Host to a variety of international tournaments, the club has eight courts (six lighted), as well as a swimming pool, an aerobics center, and a restaurant. ✉ *Rooisanto 21, Palm Beach* ☎ *297/586–0215* 🎬 *Lessons from $45*.

Water Parks

Aruba doesn't have a lot of public parks or playgrounds with swings and jungle-gym type of equipment around the tourism areas, but there are some great water-park options for a day off the resort that adults will enjoy as much as children.

★ De Palm Island Water Park

WATER SPORTS | Part of the all-inclusive program of a De Palm private island is the big colorful signature water park, which is great for all ages, including toddlers. An adults-only water park opened in late 2019, and ziplining over the park is also an option. Food and drink, snorkeling equipment, and banana boat rides are included. Free pickup and drop-off are available. ⊠ *De Palm Island Ferry Terminal, De Palm Island Way Z/N, Oranjestad* ✛ *Free water taxi from pier to the island* ☎ *297/522–4400* ⊕ *www.depalmisland. com* ☞ *From $107.*

Tarzan Boat

PARK—SPORTS-OUTDOORS | A stationary pontoon boat out in front of the RIU resorts creates a collection of climbing towers, bouncy mats, rope swings, and waterslides in the open water. Grab a pontoon boat out in front of the RIU Palace Antillas beach or get your tickets from Aruba Watersports Centre. ■**TIP**➜ **It's not very big and is more often frequented by teens and young adults doing flips off the towers than by children. Not suitable for toddlers.** ⊠ *Palm Beach* ☎ *297/569–0096* ⊕ *www.tarzanboataruba.com* 🎟 *$35.*

Windsurfing and Kiteboarding

Aruba has all it takes for windsurfing: trade winds that average 20 knots year-round (peaking May–July), a sunny climate, and perfect azure-blue waters. With a few lessons from a certified instructor, even novices will be jibing in no time. The southwestern coast's tranquil waters make it ideal for both beginners and intermediates, as the winds are steady and sudden gusts are rare. Experts will find the waters of the Atlantic, especially around Grapefield and Boca Grandi beaches, more challenging; winds are fierce and often shift without warning. Some hotels include windsurfing in their water-sports packages, and most operators can help you arrange complete windsurfing vacations.

Kiteboarding has almost overtaken windsurfing as the island's most popular wind sport to learn these days. The sport involves gliding on and above the water on a small surfboard or wakeboard while hooked up to an inflatable kite. Windsurfing experience helps, and practice time on the beach is essential, but these are different sports. You can watch the colorful kites flying all around Fisherman's Huts Beach, where boarders practice and give lessons. Pros will tell you that kiteboarding takes longer to learn, so carve out at least four hours for your first lesson on the beach. Nevertheless, once you learn how, it's easier to learn new tricks while kiteboarding.

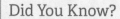

Every July sees the Hi-Winds Pro-Am Windsurfing Competition, attracting professionals and amateurs from around the world. There are divisions for women, men, juniors, masters, and grand masters. Disciplines include slalom, course racing, long distance, and freestyle. The event attracts visitors and competitors from all over the world and has become one big beach party with entertainment and additional events that go day and night.

★ Aruba Active Vacations

WATER SPORTS | FAMILY | Located near Fishermen's Huts—the best spot on the island for optimum wind and wave conditions—this operation has been the go-to for many years as THE best place to learn windsurfing, and, more recently, kiteboarding. Local alums of their school include world-class competitors like Women's Windsurf Champion Sarah-Quita Offringa, and their expert instructors ensure even first-timers are riding the waves in no time. They also offer mountain biking and stand-up paddleboarding, and they are the only outfit on the island that does "blokarting"—sail-powered land carting. ⊠ *L. G. Smith Blvd. 486, Palm Beach* ⊹ *Near Fisherman's Huts* ☎ *297/586–0989* ⊕ *www.aruba-active-vacations. com* ⊟ *From $50.*

Vela Aruba

AEROBICS/YOGA | FAMILY | All kinds of sporty fun-in-the-sun options are available at this fun and funky kiosk in the sand, including professional windsurfing and kiteboarding lessons. You can rent sea kayaks and stand-up paddleboards (and take lessons in both; instructors even offer yoga on stand-up paddleboards) and they also have zayaking, which combines the best of snorkeling and kayaking in one cool floating contraption that lets you see underwater through a screen while you float. But if you'd rather plant your feet in the sand to do your yoga, you can do that, too. ⊠ *L. G. Smith Blvd. 101, Palm Beach* ⊹ *Between the Aruba Marriott and the Ritz-Carlton* ☎ *297/586–3735* ⊕ *www.velaaruba.com* ⊟ *Rentals from $35, lessons from $60.*

INDEX

A

Addresses, *33*
Adventure tours, *59*
Aerobics, *198*
Air travel, *34–35, 51*
Alfie's in Aruba (bar), *77*
Alhambra Casino, *89*
Alto Vista Chapel, *129–130*
Amsterdam Manor Beach Resort ⊡, *24, 98*
Antesala Cafe ✕, *140*
Apartment and house rentals, *45*
Aqua Grill ✕, *113*
Arashi Beach, *14, 16, 130*
Arikok National Park and environs, *10, 14, 21, 154–166, 185*
beaches, 157, 160
children, 157, 162–163
dining, 154, 161, 166
transportation, 154
visitor information, 157
Arikok Visitor Center, *157*
Arts, *47*
Aruba Aloe Museum & Factory, *63, 65*
Aruba Active Vacations, *180, 198*
Aruba Art Fair, *60, 139, 146*
Aruba Beach Club ⊡, *98–99*
Aruba E-Bike Tours, *57*
Aruba Fairy Tales Weddings, *52*
Aruba Hi-Winds, *60*
Aruba Hotel & Tourism Association, *51*
Aruba I Do Day, *60*
Aruba International Regatta, *60*
Aruba Linear Park, *65*
Aruba Marriott Resort & Stellaris Casino ⊡, *118*

Aruba Ocean Villas ⊡, *18, 151*
Aruba Open Beach Tennis Championships, *60*
Aruba Ostrich Farm, *25, 154, 162–163*
Aruba Outdoor Adventures, *186–187*
Aruba Tourism Authority, *51–52*
Aruba Walking Tours, *57*
Aruba Water Park, *163*
Aruba Watersports Center, *191*
Aruhiba Cigars, *125*
Asi es mi Peru ✕, *94*
Atardi ✕, *113*
Atlantis Submarine, *25, 193*
ATMs, *46*
ATV tours, *20–21*
Ayo and Casibari Rock Formations, *154, 163*
Azia Restaurant Lounge ✕, *113*

B

Baby Beach, *16, 138, 142–143*
Baccarat, *169–170*
Bachelor's Beach, *143*
Bagels & Burgers ✕, *106*
Balashi Brewery and Beer Garden ✕, *65*
Banks, *46*
Barcelo Aruba ⊡, *118–119*
Barefoot ✕, *71*
Bar-hopping buses, *12*
Bavaria Food & Beer ✕, *113–114*
BAZ-RRR Galleria & Brasserie ✕, *71*
Beaches, *9, 16–17, 24–25, 39, 62, 70, 91, 94, 112–113,*

130–131, 142–143, 148–149, 157, 160
Bed in Aruban Country-side ⊡, *151*
Bicycling and motor-cycling, *20, 35, 51, 57–58, 178–180*
Birdwatching Aruba, *180*
Bis Marketplace ✕, *73*
Bistro De Suikertuin ✕, *71*
Black Beach, *190*
Blackjack, *171–172*
Blowkarting, *20*
BLT Steak ✕, *114*
BLUE (bar), *77*
Blue Residences ⊡, *99*
Boardwalk Small Hotel Aruba ⊡, *119*
Boat tours, *58–59, 181–183, 188–189*
Boca Catalina, *17, 130*
Boca Grandi, *143*
Boca Prins, *157, 160*
Boca Prins Bar & Restaurant ✕, *161*
Bon Bini Festival, *60, 79*
Boolchand's Digital World (shop), *82*
Bowling, *180–181*
Brickell Bay Beach Club & Spa Boutique Hotel ⊡, *119*
Bright Bakery ✕, *166*
Bubali Bird Sanctuary, *107*
Bubali Bliss Studios ⊡, *99*
Bucuti & Tara Beach Resort ⊡, *18, 99–100*
Bugaloe Bar & Grill, *122*
Bus travel, *35–36, 51*
Bushiribana Gold Mine Ruins, *163*
Butterfly Farm, *107, 110*

PHOTO CREDITS

Front Cover: Littleny/Alamy [Description: Example of vibrant and colorful Dutch architecture on buildings in Caribbean city of downtown Oranjestad, Aruba.]. **Back cover, from left to right:** TIERRA DEL SOL, littlenySTOCK/Shutterstock, Chiyacat/Shutterstock. **Spine:** Vilainecrevette/Shutterstock. **Interior, from left to right:** MasterPhoto/Shutterstock (1). David Troeger/Aruba Tourism Authority (2-3). **Chapter 1: Experience Aruba:** Aruba Tourism Authority (6-7). littlenySTOCK/shutterstock (8). Corey Weiner/Red Square, Inc. (9). Eagle Beach #3 by Göran Ingman (9). Jack Jackson/agefotostock (10). Aruba Tourism Authority (10). ARTN Photography (10). Aruba Tourism Authority (10). Aruba Tourism Authority (11). Aruba Tourism Authority (11). Rebecca Genin/Aruba Tourism (12). Aruba Tourism Authority (12). Passions on the Beach (12). Courtesy of Kukoo Kunuku (12). Aruba Tourism Authority (13). Vilainecrevette/Shutterstock (13). Aruba Tourism Authority (16). Jetlag Creative Studio (16). ARTN Photography (16). Aruba Tourism Authority (16). Aruba Tourism Authority (17). Kenny Theysen/Aruba Ocean Villas (18). Don Riddle Images 2013 All Rights Reserved (18). Bucuti & Tara Beach Resort (18). Divi Aruba Phoenix Beach Resort (18). Hilton (19). Aruba Tourism Authority (20). Cado de Lannoy/Aruba Active Vacations (20). TIERRA DEL SOL (20). Aruba Tourism Authority (20). Aruba Tourism Authority (21). Hans Wagemaker/Shutterstock (30). **Chapter 3: Oranjestad:** dbvirago/iStockphoto (61). Birdiegal/Shutterstock (67). Donaldford/Dreamstime (68-69). Kenneth Theysen/Timeless-Pixx (72). littlenySTOCK/Shutterstock (80). madmack66/Flickr (84). **Chapter 4: Manchebo, Druif, and Eagle Beaches:** Kjorgen/Dreamstime (87). Famke Backx/iStockphoto (92-93). Amsterdam Manor Beach Resort Aruba (98). Bucuti Beach Resort (100). **Chapter 5: Palm Beach and Noord and Western Tip (California Dunes):** DiegoMariottini/Shutterstock (105). Madame Janette's (116). Corey Weiner/redsquarephoto.com/Marriott (120). Aruba Tourism Authority (128). Sarah Bossert/iStockphoto (131). littlenySTOCK/Shutterstock (134-135). **Chapter 6: San Nicolas and Savaneta:** Aruba Tourism Authority (137). Aruba Tourism Authority (141). Kjersti Joergensen/Shutterstock (144). Steve Photography/Shutterstock (150). **Chapter 7: Arikok National Park and Environs:** Aruba Tourism Authority (153). Aruba Tourism Authority (161). Aruba Tourism Authority (162). Paul D'Innocenzo (164-165). **Chapter 8: Casinos:** Aruba Tourism Authority (167). **Chapter 9: Activities:** Steve Photography/Shutterstock (177). Corey Weiner/redsquarephoto.com/Marriott (179). Corey Weiner/redsquarephoto.com/Marriott (183). Marriott (187). Rebecca Genin/Aruba Tourism (189). Armando Goedgedrag (194-195). Paul D'Innocenzo2009 (197). **About Our Writers:** All photos are courtesy of the writers.

*Every effort has been made to trace the copyright holders, and we apologize in advance for any accidental errors. We would be happy to apply the corrections in the following printing of this publication.

About Our Writer

Sue Campbell is an award-winning travel-and-lifestyle writer specializing in the Dutch Caribbean. She has hundreds of articles to her credit about Aruba, Bonaire, Curaçao, and St. Maarten in over 22 major national and international print and Web outlets as well as on-island magazines. When Susan isn't seeking the best hot spots in the tropics, she is reporting about the highlights of her hometown in Montreal. She updated the entire Aruba guide, as well as the Aruba, Bonaire, Curaçao, and Saba content of *Fodor's Essential Caribbean 2nd*.

Fodor's InFocus ARUBA

Publisher: Stephen Horowitz, *General Manager*

Editorial: Douglas Stallings, *Editorial Director;* Jacinta O'Halloran, Amanda Sadlowski, *Senior Editors;* Kayla Becker, Alexis Kelly, Teddy Minford, Rachael Roth, *Editors*

Design: Tina Malaney, *Design and Production Director;* Jessica Gonzalez, *Graphic Designer;* Mariana Tabares, *Design & Production Intern*

Production: Jennifer DePrima, *Editorial Production Manager;* Carrie Parker, *Senior Production Editor;* Elyse Rozelle, *Production Editor;* Jackson Pranica, *Editorial Production Assistant*

Maps: Rebecca Baer, *Senior Map Editor;* David Lindroth, with additional cartography provided by Henry Columb, Mark Stroud, and Ali Baird, Moon Street Cartography, *Cartographers*

Photography: Viviane Teles, *Senior Photo Editor;* Namrata Aggarwal, Ashok Kumar, Carl Yu, *Photo Editors;* Rebecca Rimmer, *Photo Intern*

Business & Operations: Chuck Hoover, *Chief Marketing Officer;* Robert Ames, *Group General Manager;* Tara McCrillis, *Director of Publishing Operations;* Victor Bernal, *Business Analyst*

Public Relations and Marketing: Joe Ewaskiw, *Senior Director Communications & Public Relations;* Esther Su, *Senior Marketing Manager*

Fodors.com: Jeremy Tarr, *Editorial Director;* Rachael Levitt, *Managing Editor*

Technology: Jon Atkinson, *Director of Technology;* Rudresh Teotia, *Lead Developer;* Jacob Ashpis, *Content Operations Manager*

Writers: Sue Campbell
Editor: Alexis Kelly
Production Editor: Jennifer DePrima

7th Edition

ISBN 978-1-64097-225-4

ISSN 1939–988X

SPECIAL SALES

This book is available at special discounts for bulk purchases for sales promotions or premiums. For more information, e-mail SpecialMarkets@fodors.com.

PRINTED IN CANADA

10 9 8 7 6 5 4 3 2 1

NOTES

NOTES